Mastering C# Concurrency

Create robust and scalable applications, along with responsive UI, using concurrency and the multi-threading infrastructure in .NET and C#

Eugene Agafonov

Andrew Koryavchenko

professional expertise distilled

PUBLISHING

BIRMINGHAM - MUMBAI

Mastering C# Concurrency

First published: October 2015

Production reference: 1231015

Published by Packt Publishing Ltd.
Livery Place
35 Livery Street
Birmingham B3 2PB, UK.

ISBN 978-1-78528-665-0

www.packtpub.com

Credits

Authors
Eugene Agafonov
Andrew Koryavchenko

Reviewers
Tim Gabrhel
Michael Berantzino Hansen
Güray Özen
Simon Soanes

Acquisition Editor
Reshma Raman

Content Development Editor
Zeeyan Pinheiro

Technical Editor
Menza Mathew

Copy Editors
Kausambhi Majumdar
Alpha Singh

Project Coordinator
Suzanne Coutinho

Proofreader
Safis Editing

Indexer
Rekha Nair

Production Coordinator
Melwyn Dsa

Cover Work
Melwyn Dsa

About the Authors

Eugene Agafonov leads the Lingvo Live development department at ABBYY, and he lives and works in Moscow. He has over 15 years of professional experience in software development and has been working with C# ever since it was in beta version. He has been a Microsoft MVP in ASP.NET since 2006, and he often speaks at local software development conferences, such as DevCon Russia, about cutting-edge technologies in modern web and server-side application development. His main professional interests are cloud-based software architecture, scalability, and reliability. Eugene is a huge fan of football and plays the guitar with a local rock band. You can reach him at his personal blog at eugeneagafonov.com or his Twitter handle at @eugene_agafonov.

He also wrote *Multithreading in C# 5.0 Cookbook* by Packt Publishing.

I would like to thank Sergey Teplyakov, who is a super cool Microsoft guy and has an ultimate twitter account at @STeplyakov, for helping me a lot in writing chapters 6 and 7, and his invaluable advice that allowed me to make this book better.

Andrew Koryavchenko is a software developer and an architect who lives in Moscow, Russia. He is one of the founders of rsdn.ru — the largest Russian software developers' community portal.

His specialty is ERP systems and developer tools. He participated in ReSharper Visual Studio extension development, which is a well-known productivity tool for .NET developers. Currently, he is working on parsing and compilation tools for .NET development and also supports and develops the rsdn.ru portal.

Andrew regularly speaks at online and offline events and conferences dedicated to Microsoft technologies, and he publishes articles on software development topics. He also used to teach Enterprise Software Development course in Kuban State University.

Andrew has been a Microsoft MVP in C# since 2005.

About the Reviewers

Tim Gabrhel is a senior application developer at Concurrency Inc., with a core focus on Microsoft Azure and modern .NET technologies. He is a creator and maker and loves being hands-on with new technologies and making them work in real life. Tim has been a consultant for Fortune 100 companies. He has contributed to the architecture and key components of enterprise solutions that have reached hundreds of thousands of users around the world. You can follow Tim and his technical journey at his blog, `http://timgabrhel.com`.

Michael Berantzino Hansen is a MCPD .NET Enterprise Application Developer specializing in high performance and efficient frameworks. He has been programming since the mid 80s from the age of 9. He started with Basic and then moved on to C++. In 1999, he earned a bachelors degree in computer science, economics, and organizational development, while working part time for ground-breaking startups. In 2005, he moved on to C# as his preferred platform. Michael excels in developing complex frameworks, algorithms, and applications. He does full stack development using modern technologies. He recently adopted TypeScript as his preferred platform for client-side web development.

Michael currently works as a chief system developer in the SPAMfighter, developing complex e-mail analysis platforms responsible for all enterprise solutions in SPAMfighter.

Güray Özen has been working as a research fellow in the programming models team at Barcelona Supercomputing Center (BSC) since August 2013. His work is also part of his PhD research that explores compiler-based parallelism and optimizations for heterogeneous systems. Besides this, his current research interests consist of the principles of programming languages and parallel programming. He received a master's degree in high performance computing from the Department of Computer Architecture at Universitat Politècnica de Catalunya – BarcelonaTech in 2014. In 2010 and 2012, he worked at one of the biggest banks in Turkey as a C#-backed applications developer. He has a bachelor's degree in computer science engineering from Dokuz Eylul Univeristy in Izmir, Turkey.

Simon Soanes is a software developer with a background in networking technologies, databases, distributed systems, and debugging. Ever since the days of the C64, he has enjoyed writing software, playing computer games, and making devices communicate with each other in creative ways.

He's currently working in the south of England as a contractor. At some point, he became addicted to solving technical problems and automating things.

He occasionally writes a blog at http://www.nullify.net/.

www.PacktPub.com

Support files, eBooks, discount offers, and more

For support files and downloads related to your book, please visit www.PacktPub.com.

Did you know that Packt offers eBook versions of every book published, with PDF and ePub files available? You can upgrade to the eBook version at www.PacktPub.com and as a print book customer, you are entitled to a discount on the eBook copy. Get in touch with us at service@packtpub.com for more details.

At www.PacktPub.com, you can also read a collection of free technical articles, sign up for a range of free newsletters and receive exclusive discounts and offers on Packt books and eBooks.

https://www2.packtpub.com/books/subscription/packtlib

Do you need instant solutions to your IT questions? PacktLib is Packt's online digital book library. Here, you can search, access, and read Packt's entire library of books.

Why subscribe?

- Fully searchable across every book published by Packt
- Copy and paste, print, and bookmark content
- On demand and accessible via a web browser

Free access for Packt account holders

If you have an account with Packt at www.PacktPub.com, you can use this to access PacktLib today and view 9 entirely free books. Simply use your login credentials for immediate access.

Instant updates on new Packt books

Get notified! Find out when new books are published by following @PacktEnterprise on Twitter or the *Packt Enterprise* Facebook page.

To Mom and Dad — you are the best parents on Earth and I love you so much.

Table of Contents

Preface   **v**

Chapter 1: Traditional Concurrency   **1**

What's the problem?   **2**
Using locks   **5**
    Lock statement   5
    Monitor class   9
Reader-writer lock   **12**
Spin lock   **19**
    Thread.SpinWait   19
    System.Threading.SpinWait   19
    System.Threading.SpinLock   20
Optimization strategy   **22**
    Lock localization   22
    Shared data minimization   23
Summary   **26**

Chapter 2: Lock-Free Concurrency   **27**

Memory model and compiler optimizations   **28**
The System.Threading.Interlocked class   **30**
Interlocked internals   **33**
Writing lock-free code   **34**
    The ABA problem   35
    The lock-free stack   37
    The lock-free queue   43
Summary   **49**

Chapter 3: Understanding Parallelism Granularity   51

The number of threads   51
Using the thread pool   58
Understanding granularity   60
Choosing the coarse-grained or fine-grained approach   64
Summary   65

Chapter 4: Task Parallel Library in Depth   67

Task composition   68
Tasks hierarchy   73
Awaiting task completion   75
Task cancellation   76
    Checking a flag   78
    Throwing an exception   79
    Using OS wait objects with WaitHandle   80
    Cancellation using callbacks   81
Latency and the coarse-grained approach with TPL   83
Exception handling   87
Using the Parallel class   90
    Parallel.Invoke   91
    Parallel.For and Parallel.Foreach   92
    Understanding the task scheduler   93
Summary   97

Chapter 5: C# Language Support for Asynchrony   99

Implementing the downloading of images from Bing   99
    Creating a simple synchronous solution   100
    Creating a parallel solution with Task Parallel Library   105
    Enhancing the code with C# 5.0 built-in support for asynchrony   108
    Simulating C# asynchronous infrastructure with iterators   110
Is the async keyword really needed?   113
Fire-and-forget tasks   113
Other useful TPL features   114
    Task.Delay   115
    Task.Yield   115
Implementing a custom awaitable type   115
Summary   117

Chapter 6: Using Concurrent Data Structures — 119

Standard collections and synchronization primitives — 120
Implementing a cache with ReaderWriterLockSlim — 121
Concurrent collections in .NET — 124
ConcurrentDictionary — 125
  Using Lazy<T> — 128
  Implementation details — 129
    Lock-free operations — 131
    Fine-grained lock operations — 132
    Exclusive lock operations — 134
  Using the implementation details in practice — 136
ConcurrentBag<T> — 136
  ConcurrentBag in practice — 139
ConcurrentQueue<T> — 140
ConcurrentStack<T> — 143
The Producer/Consumer pattern — 143
  Custom Producer/Consumer pattern implementation — 144
The Producer/Consumer pattern in .NET 4.0+ — 149
Summary — 152

Chapter 7: Leveraging Parallel Patterns — 155

Concurrent idioms — 155
  Process Tasks in Completion Order — 155
  Limiting the parallelism degree — 158
  Setting a task timeout — 162
Asynchronous patterns — 163
  Asynchronous Programming Model — 164
  Event-based Asynchronous Pattern — 167
  Task-based Asynchronous Pattern — 171
Concurrent patterns — 173
  Parallel pipelines — 174
Summary — 179

Chapter 8: Server-Side Asynchrony — 181

Server applications — 181
The OWIN Web API framework — 183
Load testing and scalability — 187
I/O and CPU-bound tasks — 191
Deep dive into asynchronous I/O — 194
Real and fake asynchronous I/O operations — 198
Synchronization context — 203
CPU-bound tasks and queues — 206
Summary — 207

Chapter 9: Concurrency in the User Interface   **209**

The importance of asynchrony for UI   **209**

UI threads and message loops   **210**

Common problems and solutions   **216**

How the await keyword works   **220**

Execution and synchronization contexts   221

Performance issues   **223**

Summary   **229**

Chapter 10: Troubleshooting Parallel Programs   **231**

How troubleshooting parallel programs is different   **231**

Heisenbugs   232

Writing tests   **232**

Load tests   233

Unit tests   233

Integration tests   **239**

Debugging   **244**

Just my code setting   244

Call stack window   245

Threads window   246

Tasks window   247

Parallel stacks window   248

Performance measurement and profiling   **250**

The Concurrency Visualizer   250

Summary   **254**

Index   **255**

Preface

Recent C# and .NET developments involve implicitly using asynchrony and concurrency, even when you are not aware of them. This can lead to further problems since many details are usually hidden inside the C# language infrastructure and the .NET base class library APIs. To avoid problems and to be able to create robust applications, a developer has to know exactly what is going on under the hood of asynchrony in .NET.

Besides this, it is important to understand your goals when writing a concurrent application. If it is running on the client, it is usually a good thing to use all the computational resources available so that the application becomes as fast as possible. This involves effective multiple CPU cores usage, and thus requires parallel programming skills. However, if the application is running on the server, it is more important that the server supports as many clients as possible, than the performance of a concrete client request processing. This requires a programmer to distinguish asynchrony from multithreading and have an understanding of scalability.

All these topics will be covered in this book, providing you with enough information to achieve a solid understanding of asynchronous and parallel programming in C#. We will start with basic multithreading concepts, review common concurrent programming problems and solutions, and then we will go through C# and .NET support for writing concurrent applications. Further in the book, we will cover concurrent data structures and patterns, and we will review client-side and server-side concurrency issues. At the end of the book, we will outline the basic principles for creating robust concurrent programs.

What this book covers

Chapter 1, Traditional Concurrency, covers common problems with multithreading and solutions to these problems. You will refresh your knowledge about basic locking techniques and how to make locking more efficient.

Chapter 2, Lock-Free Concurrency, goes further into performance optimization. It covers various ways to write concurrent programs without locking, making the code fast and reliable.

Chapter 3, Understanding Parallelism Granularity, explains another important aspect of organizing your parallel code—splitting a computational workload between threads. It introduces coarse-grained and fine-grained approaches, showing their pros and cons.

Chapter 4, Task Parallel Library in Depth, goes into the details of Task Parallel Library—a framework to organize your concurrent program as a set of related tasks. You will find the internals of TPL reviewed and explained.

Chapter 5, C# Language Support for Asynchrony, is a deep dive into the C# language infrastructure. The chapter shows exactly how the async and await keywords work and how you can write your own await-compatible code.

Chapter 6, Using Concurrent Data Structures, covers the use of data structures in a concurrent program in detail, including standard .NET concurrent collections and custom thread safe collections implementations.

Chapter 7, Leveraging Parallel Patterns, reviews programming patterns related to parallel applications. The chapter describes different kinds of patterns—historical .NET idioms, useful code snippets, and a high-level parallel pipeline pattern.

Chapter 8, Server-Side Asynchrony, is a solution description to the problem of using asynchrony on the server. It explains why it is very important to distinguish asynchrony from parallelism, and how it can affect the scalability and reliability of your server.

Chapter 9, Concurrency in the User Interface, describes the details of how the user interface is implemented, what a message loop is, and why it is very important to keep the UI thread nonblocked.

Chapter 10, Troubleshooting Parallel Programs, explains how to find out what is wrong with your parallel program. You will learn how to write unit tests for an asynchronous code, how to debug it, and find performance bottlenecks.

What you need for this book

You will need Visual Studio 2013 or 2015 to run the code samples. For most of the chapters, it will be enough to use the free Visual Studio Community 2013/2015 editions, but the performance test samples will require the Test/Ultimate or Enterprise editions. However, if you cannot use this, it is possible to download the free Apache bench tool to run performance tests as described in the book.

Who this book is for

Mastering C# Concurrency is written for existing C# developers who have a knowledge of basic multithreading concepts and want to improve their asynchronous and parallel programming skills. The book covers different topics, from basic concepts to complicated programming patterns and algorithms using the C# and .NET ecosystems. This will be useful to server and client developers, because it covers all the important aspects of using concurrency and asynchrony on both sides.

Conventions

In this book, you will find a number of styles of text that distinguish between different kinds of information. Here are some examples of these styles, and an explanation of their meaning.

Code words in text, database table names, folder names, filenames, file extensions, pathnames, dummy URLs, user input, and Twitter handles are shown as follows: "This happens because the Add method of the List<T> class is not thread safe, and the reason for this lies in the implementation details."

A block of code is set as follows:

```
public void Add(T item)
{
    if (_size == _items.Length) EnsureCapacity(_size + 1);
    _items[_size++] = item;
    _version++;
}
```

When we wish to draw your attention to a particular part of a code block, the relevant lines or items are set in bold:

```
public void Add(T item)
{
    if (_size == _items.Length) EnsureCapacity(_size + 1);
    _items[_size++] = item;
    _version++;
}
```

Any command-line input or output is written as follows:

```
T2: Add - [T2]: Item 1
T1: Add - [T1]: Item 1
T2: Add - [T2]: Item 2
T2: Add - [T2]: Item 3
```

New terms and important words are shown in bold. Words that you see on the screen, in menus or dialog boxes for example, appear in the text like this: "Click on **Finish** and repeat all this for another controller."

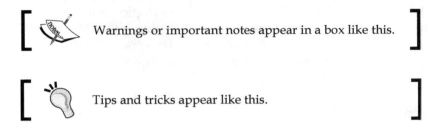

Warnings or important notes appear in a box like this.

Tips and tricks appear like this.

Reader feedback

Feedback from our readers is always welcome. Let us know what you think about this book—what you liked or may have disliked. Reader feedback is important for us to develop titles that you really get the most out of.

To send us general feedback, simply send an e-mail to feedback@packtpub.com, and mention the book title via the subject of your message.

If there is a topic that you have expertise in and you are interested in either writing or contributing to a book, see our author guide on www.packtpub.com/authors.

Customer support

Now that you are the proud owner of a Packt book, we have a number of things to help you to get the most from your purchase.

Downloading the example code

You can download the example code files for all Packt books you have purchased from your account at http://www.packtpub.com. If you purchased this book elsewhere, you can visit http://www.packtpub.com/support and register to have the files e-mailed directly to you.

Errata

Although we have taken every care to ensure the accuracy of our content, mistakes do happen. If you find a mistake in one of our books—maybe a mistake in the text or the code—we would be grateful if you would report this to us. By doing so, you can save other readers from frustration and help us improve subsequent versions of this book. If you find any errata, please report them by visiting http://www.packtpub.com/submit-errata, selecting your book, clicking on the **errata submission form** link, and entering the details of your errata. Once your errata are verified, your submission will be accepted and the errata will be uploaded on our website, or added to any list of existing errata, under the Errata section of that title. Any existing errata can be viewed by selecting your title from http://www.packtpub.com/support.

Piracy

Piracy of copyright material on the Internet is an ongoing problem across all media. At Packt, we take the protection of our copyright and licenses very seriously. If you come across any illegal copies of our works, in any form, on the Internet, please provide us with the location address or website name immediately so that we can pursue a remedy.

Please contact us at copyright@packtpub.com with a link to the suspected pirated material.

We appreciate your help in protecting our authors, and our ability to bring you valuable content.

Questions

You can contact us at questions@packtpub.com if you are having a problem with any aspect of the book, and we will do our best to address it.

1
Traditional Concurrency

Speaking of concurrency, we have to start talking about threads. Ironically, the reason behind implementing threads was to isolate programs from each other. Back in the early days of Windows, versions 3.* used **cooperative multitasking**. This meant that the operating system executed all the programs on a single execution loop, and if one of those programs hung, every other program and the operating system itself would stop responding as well and then it would be required to reboot the machine to resolve this problem.

To create a more robust environment, the OS had to learn how to give every program its own piece of CPU, so if one program entered an infinite loop, the others would still be able to use the CPU for their own needs. A thread is an implementation of this concept. The threads allow implementing **preemptive multitasking**, where instead of the application deciding when to yield control to another application, the OS controls how much CPU time to give to each application.

When CPUs started to have multiple cores, it became more beneficial to make full use of the computational capability available. The use of the threads directly by applications suddenly became more worthwhile. However, when exploring multithreading issues, such as how to share the data between the threads safely, the set-up time of the threads immediately become evident.

In this chapter, we will consider the basic concurrent programming pitfalls and the traditional approach to deal with them.

What's the problem?

Simply using multiple threads in a program is not a very complicated task. If your program can be easily separated into several independent tasks, then you just run them in different threads, and these threads can be scaled along with the number of CPU cores. However, usually real world programs require some interaction between these threads, such as exchanging information to coordinate their work. This cannot be implemented without sharing some data, which requires allocating some RAM space in such a way that it is accessible from all the threads. Dealing with this shared state is the root of almost every problem related to parallel programming.

The first common problem with shared state is undefined access order. If we have read and write access, this leads to incorrect calculation results. This situation is commonly referred to as a **race condition**.

Following is a sample of a race condition. We have a counter, which is being changed from different threads simultaneously. Each thread increments the counter, then does some work, and then decrements the counter.

```
const int iterations = 10000;
var counter = 0;
ThreadStart proc = () => {
    for (int i = 0; i < iterations; i++) {
        counter++;
        Thread.SpinWait(100);
        counter--;
    }
};
var threads = Enumerable
    .Range(0, 8)
    .Select(n => new Thread(proc))
    .ToArray();
foreach (var thread in threads)
  thread.Start();
foreach (var thread in threads)
  thread.Join();
Console.WriteLine(counter);
```

The expected counter value is 0. However, when you run the program, you get different numbers (which is usually not 0, but it could be) each time. The reason is that incrementing and decrementing the counter is not an atomic operation, but consists of three separate steps – reading the counter value, incrementing or decrementing this value, and writing the result back into the counter.

Let us assume that we have initial counter value 0, and two threads. The first thread reads 0, increments it to 1, and writes 1 into the counter. The second thread reads 1 from the counter, increments it to 2, and then writes 2 into the counter. This seems to be correct and is exactly what we expected. This scenario is represented in the following diagram:

Thread A	read counter: 0	0+1=1	write 1 into counter		
Counter	0	0	1	1	2
Thread B			read counter: 1	1+1=2	write 2 into counter

 Now the first thread reads 2 from the counter, and at the same time it decrements it to 1; the second thread reads 2 from the counter, because the first thread hasn't written 1 into the counter yet. So now, the first thread writes 1 into the counter, and the second thread decrements 2 to 1 and writes the value 1 into the counter. As a result, we have the value 1, while we're expecting 0. This scenario is represented in the following diagram:

Thread A	read counter: 2	2-1=1	write 1 into counter		
Counter	2	2	1	1	1
Thread B			read counter: 2	2-1=1	write 1 into counter

Downloading the example code

You can download the example code files from your account at http://www.packtpub.com for all the Packt Publishing books you have purchased. If you purchased this book elsewhere, you can visit http://www.packtpub.com/support and register to have the files e-mailed directly to you.

To avoid this, we have to restrict access to the counter so that only one thread reads it at a time, calculates the result, and writes it back. Such a restriction is called a lock. However, by using it to resolve a race condition problem, we create other possibilities for our concurrent code to fail. With such a restriction, we turn our parallel process into a sequential process, which in turn means that our code runs less efficiently. The more time the code runs inside the lock, the less efficient and scalable the whole program is. This is because the lock held by one thread blocks the other threads from performing their work, thereby making the whole program take longer to run. So, we have to minimize the lock time to keep the other threads running, instead of waiting for the lock to be released to start doing their calculations.

Another problem related to locks is best illustrated by the following example. It shows two threads using two resources, A and B. The first thread needs to lock object A first, then B, while the second thread starts with locking B and then A.

```
const int count = 10000;

var a = new object();
var b = new object();
var thread1 =
  new Thread(
    () =>
    {
      for (int i = 0; i < count; i++)
        lock (a)
          lock (b)
            Thread.SpinWait(100);
    });
var thread2 =
  new Thread(
    () =>
    {
      for (int i = 0; i < count; i++)
        lock (b)
          lock (a)
            Thread.SpinWait(100);
    });

thread1.Start();
thread2.Start();
thread1.Join();
thread2.Join();
Console.WriteLine("Done");
```

It looks like this code is alright, but if you run it several times, it will eventually hang. The reason for this lies in an issue with the locking order. If the first thread locks A, and the second locks B before the first thread does, then the second thread starts waiting for the lock on A to be released. However, to release the lock on A, the first thread needs to put a lock on B, which is already locked by the second thread. Therefore, both the threads will wait forever and the program will hang.

Such a situation is called a **deadlock**. It is usually quite hard to diagnose deadlocks, because it is hard to reproduce one.

 The best way to avoid deadlocks is to take preventive measures when writing code. The best practice is to avoid complicated lock structures and nested locks, and minimize the time in locks. If you suspect there could be a deadlock, then there is another way to prevent it from happening, which is by setting a timeout for acquiring a lock.

Using locks

There are different types of locks in C# and .NET. We will cover these later in the chapter, and also throughout the book. Let us start with the most common way to use a lock in C#, which is a `lock` statement.

Lock statement

Lock statement in C# uses a single argument, which could be an instance of any class. This instance will represent the lock itself.

Reading other people's codes, you could see that a lock uses the instance of collection or class, which contains shared data. It is not a good practice, because someone else could use this object for locking, and potentially create a deadlock situation. So, it is recommended to use a special private synchronization object, the sole purpose of which is to serve as a concrete lock:

```
// Bad
lock(myCollection) {
  myCollection.Add(data);
}

// Good
lock(myCollectionLock) {
  myCollection.Add(data);
}
```

It is dangerous to use `lock(this)` and `lock(typeof(MyType))`. The basic idea why it is bad remains the same: the objects you are locking could be publicly accessible, and thus someone else could acquire a lock on it causing a deadlock. However, using the `this` keyword makes the situation more implicit; if someone else made the object public, it would be very hard to track that it is being used inside a lock.

Locking the type object is even worse. In the current versions of .NET, the runtime type objects could be shared across application domains (running in the same process). It is possible because those objects are immutable. However, this means that a deadlock could be caused, not only by another thread, but also by ANOTHER APPLICATION, and I bet that you would hardly understand what's going on in such a case.

Following is how we can rewrite the first example with race condition and fix it using C# lock statement. Now the code will be as follows:

```
const int iterations = 10000;
var counter = 0;
var lockFlag = new object();
ThreadStart proc = () => {
  for (int i = 0; i < iterations; i++)
  {
    lock (lockFlag)
      counter++;
    Thread.SpinWait(100);
    lock (lockFlag)
      counter--;
  }
};
var threads = Enumerable
  .Range(0, 8)
  .Select(n => new Thread(proc))
  .ToArray();
foreach (var thread in threads)
  thread.Start();
foreach (var thread in threads)
  thread.Join();
Console.WriteLine(counter);
```

Now this code works properly, and the result is always 0.

To understand what is happening when a lock statement is used in the program, let us look at the Intermediate Language code, which is a result of compiling C# program. Consider the following C# code:

```
static void Main()
{
  var ctr = 0;
  var lockFlag = new object();
  lock (lockFlag)
    ctr++;
}
```

The preceding block of code will be compiled into the following:

```
.method private hidebysig static void  Main() cil managed {
  .entrypoint
  // Code size       48 (0x30)
  .maxstack  2
  .locals init ([0] int32 ctr,
                [1] object lockFlag,
                [2] bool '<>s__LockTaken0',
                [3] object CS$2$0000,
                [4] bool CS$4$0001)
  IL_0000:  nop
  IL_0001:  ldc.i4.0
  IL_0002:  stloc.0
  IL_0003:  newobj      instance void [mscorlib]System.Object::.ctor()
  IL_0008:  stloc.1
  IL_0009:  ldc.i4.0
  IL_000a:  stloc.2
  .try
  {
    IL_000b:  ldloc.1
    IL_000c:  dup
    IL_000d:  stloc.3
    IL_000e:  ldloca.s    '<>s__LockTaken0'
    IL_0010:  call        void [mscorlib]System.Threading.
Monitor::Enter(object, bool&)
    IL_0015:  nop
    IL_0016:  ldloc.0
    IL_0017:  ldc.i4.1
    IL_0018:  add
    IL_0019:  stloc.0
    IL_001a:  leave.s     IL_002e
  } // end .try
  finally
```

```
  {
    IL_001c:   ldloc.2
    IL_001d:   ldc.i4.0
    IL_001e:   ceq
    IL_0020:   stloc.s     CS$4$0001
    IL_0022:   ldloc.s     CS$4$0001
    IL_0024:   brtrue.s    IL_002d
    IL_0026:   ldloc.3
    IL_0027:   call        void [mscorlib]System.Threading.
Monitor::Exit(object)
    IL_002c:   nop
    IL_002d:   endfinally
  }  // end handler
  IL_002e:   nop
  IL_002f:   ret
} // end of method Program::Main
```

This can be explained with decompilation to C#. It will look like this:

```
static void Main()
{
  var ctr = 0;
  var lockFlag = new object();
  bool lockTaken = false;

  try
  {
    System.Threading.Monitor.Enter(lockFlag, ref lockTaken);
    ctr++;
  }
  finally
  {
    if (lockTaken)
      System.Threading.Monitor.Exit(lockFlag);
  }
}
```

It turns out that the lock statement turns into calling the Monitor.Enter and Monitor.Exit methods, wrapped into a try-finally block. The Enter method acquires an exclusive lock and returns a bool value, indicating that a lock was successfully acquired. If something went wrong, for example an exception has been thrown, the bool value would be set to false, and the Exit method would release the acquired lock.

A `try-finally` block ensures that the acquired lock will be released even if an exception occurs inside the lock statement. If the `Enter` method indicates that we cannot acquire a lock, then the `Exit` method will not be executed.

Monitor class

The `Monitor` class contains other useful methods that help us to write concurrent code. One of such methods is the `TryEnter` method, which allows the provision of a timeout value to it. If a lock could not be obtained before the timeout is expired, the `TryEnter` method would return `false`. This is quite an efficient method to prevent deadlocks, but you have to write significantly more code.

Consider the previous deadlock sample refactored in a way that one of the threads uses `Monitor.TryEnter` instead of `lock`:

```
static void Main()
{
  const int count = 10000;

  var a = new object();
  var b = new object();
  var thread1 = new Thread(
    () => {
      for (int i = 0; i < count; i++)
        lock (a)
        lock (b)
        Thread.SpinWait(100);
  });
  var thread2 = new Thread(() => LockTimeout(a, b, count));
  thread1.Start();
  thread2.Start();
  thread1.Join();
  thread2.Join();
  Console.WriteLine("Done");
}

static void LockTimeout(object a, object b, int count)
{
  bool accquiredB = false;
  bool accquiredA = false;
  const int waitSeconds = 5;
  const int retryCount = 3;
  for (int i = 0; i < count; i++)
  {
    int retries = 0;
    while (retries < retryCount)
    {
```

```
        try
        {
          accquiredB = Monitor.TryEnter(b, TimeSpan.FromSeconds(
            waitSeconds));
          if (accquiredB) {
            try {
              accquiredA = Monitor.TryEnter(a, TimeSpan.FromSeconds(
                waitSeconds));
              if (accquiredA) {
                Thread.SpinWait(100);
                break;
              }
              else {
                retries++;
              }
            }
            finally {
              if (accquiredA) {
                Monitor.Exit(a);
              }
            }
          }
          else {
            retries++;
          }
        }
        finally {
          if (accquiredB)
            Monitor.Exit(b);
        }
      }
      if (retries >= retryCount)
        Console.WriteLine("could not obtain locks");
    }
  }
```

In the `LockTimeout` method, we implemented a retry strategy. For each loop iteration, we try to acquire lock B first, and if we cannot do so in 5 seconds, we try again. If we have successfully acquired lock B, then we in turn try to acquire lock A, and if we wait for it for more than 5 seconds, we try again to acquire both the locks. This guarantees that if someone waits endlessly to acquire a lock on B, then this operation will eventually succeed.

If we do not succeed acquiring lock B, then we try again for a defined number of attempts. Then either we succeed, or we admit that we cannot obtain the needed locks and go to the next iteration.

In addition, the `Monitor` class can be used to orchestrate multiple threads into a workflow with the `Wait`, `Pulse`, and `PulseAll` methods. When a main thread calls the `Wait` method, the current lock is released, and the thread is blocked until some other thread calls the `Pulse` or `PulseAll` methods. This allows the coordination the different threads execution into some sort of sequence.

A simple example of such workflow is when we have two threads: the main thread and an additional thread that performs some calculation. We would like to pause the main thread until the second thread finishes its work, and then get back to the main thread, and in turn block this additional thread until we have other data to calculate. This can be illustrated by the following code:

```
var arg = 0;
var result = "";
var counter = 0;
var lockHandle = new object();
var calcThread = new Thread(() => {
  while (true)
  lock (lockHandle)
  {
    counter++;
    result = arg.ToString();
    Monitor.Pulse(lockHandle);
    Monitor.Wait(lockHandle);
  }
})
{
  IsBackground = true
};
lock (lockHandle)
{
  calcThread.Start();
  Thread.Sleep(100);
  Console.WriteLine("counter = {0}, result = {1}", counter,
    result);

  arg = 123;
  Monitor.Pulse(lockHandle);
  Monitor.Wait(lockHandle);
  Console.WriteLine("counter = {0}, result = {1}", counter,
    result);

  arg = 321;
  Monitor.Pulse(lockHandle);
  Monitor.Wait(lockHandle);
  Console.WriteLine("counter = {0}, result = {1}", counter,
    result);
}
```

As a result of running this program, we will get the following output:

```
counter = 0, result =
counter = 1, result = 123
counter = 2, result = 321
```

At first, we start a calculation thread. Then we print the initial values for `counter` and `result`, and then we call `Pulse`. This puts the calculation thread into a queue called **ready queue**. This means that this thread is ready to acquire this lock as soon as it gets released. Then we call the `Wait` method, which releases the lock and puts the main thread into a **waiting queue**. The first thread in the ready queue, which is our calculation thread, acquires the lock and starts to work. After completing its calculations, the second thread calls `Pulse`, which moves a thread at the head of the waiting queue (which is our main thread) into the ready queue. If there are several threads in the waiting queue, only the first one would go into the ready queue. To put all the threads into the ready queue at once, we could use the `PulseAll` method. So, when the second thread calls `Wait`, our main thread reacquires the lock, changes the calculation data, and repeats the whole process one more time.

> Note that we can use the `Wait`, `Pulse`, and `PulseAll` methods only when the current thread owns a lock. The `Wait` method could block indefinitely in case no other threads call `Pulse` or `PulseAll`, so it can be a reason for a deadlock. To prevent deadlocks, we can specify a timeout value to the `Wait` method to be able to react in case we cannot reacquire the lock for a certain time period.

Reader-writer lock

It is very common to see samples of code where the shared state is one of the standard .NET collections: `List<T>` or `Dictionary<K, V>`. These collections are not thread safe; thus we need synchronization to organize concurrent access.

There are special concurrent collections that can be used instead of the standard list and dictionary to achieve thread safety. We will review them in *Chapter 6, Using Concurrent Data Structures*. For now, let us assume that we have reasons to organize concurrent access by ourselves.

The easiest way to achieve synchronization is to use the `lock` operator when reading and writing from these collections. However, the MSDN documentation states that if a collection is not modified while being read, synchronization is not required:

> *It is safe to perform multiple read operations on a List<T>, but issues can occur if the collection is modified while it's being read.*

Another important MSDN page states the following regarding a collection:

> *A Dictionary<TKey, TValue> can support multiple readers concurrently, as long as the collection is not modified.*

This means that we can perform the read operations from multiple threads if the collection is not being modified. This allows us to avoid excessive locking, and minimizes performance overhead and possible deadlocks in such situations.

To leverage this, there is a standard .NET Framework class, `System.Threading.ReaderWriterLock`. It provides three types of locks: to read something from a resource, to write something, and a special one to upgrade the reader lock to a writer lock. The following method pairs represent these locks: `AcquireReaderLock/ReleaseReaderLock`, `AcquireWriterLock/ReleaseWriterLock`, and `UpgradeToWriterLock/DowngradeFromWriterLock`, correspondingly. It is also possible to provide a timeout value, after which the request to acquire the lock will expire. Providing the `-1` value means that a lock has no timeout.

It is important to always release a lock after acquiring it. Always put the code for releasing a lock into the `finally` block of the `try/catch` statement, otherwise any exception thrown before releasing this lock would leave the `ReaderWriterLock` object in a locked state, preventing any further access to this lock.

A reader lock puts a thread in the blocked state only when there is at least one writer lock acquired. Otherwise, no real thread blocking happens. A writer lock waits until every other lock is released, and then in turn it prevents the acquiring of any other locks, until it's released.

Upgrading a lock is useful; when inside an open reader lock, we need to write something into a collection. For example, we first check if there is an entry with some key in the dictionary, and insert this entry if it does not exist. Acquiring a writer lock would be inefficient, since there could be no write operation, so it is optimal to use this upgrade scenario.

Note that using any kind of lock is still not as efficient as a simple check, and it makes sense to use patterns such as double-checked locking. Consider the follow code snippet:

```
if (writeRequiredCondition)
{
  _rwLock.AcquireWriterLock();
  try
  {
    if (writeRequiredCondition)
      // do write
  }
  finally
  {
    _rwLock.ReleaseWriterLock();
  }
}
```

The `ReaderWriterLock` class has a nested locks counter, and it avoids creating a new lock when trying to acquire it when inside another lock. In such a case, the lock counter is incremented and then decremented when the nested lock is released. The real lock is acquired only when this counter is equal to to 0.

Nevertheless, this implementation has some serious drawbacks. First, it uses thread blocking, which is quite performance costly, and besides that, adds its own additional overhead. In addition, if the write operation is very short, then using `ReaderWriterLock` could be even worse than simply locking the collection for every operation. In addition to that, the method names and semantics are not intuitive, which makes reading and understanding the code much harder.

This is the reason why the new implementation, `System.Threading. ReaderWriterLockSlim`, was introduced in .NET Framework 3.5. It should *always* be used instead of `ReaderWriterLock` for the following reasons:

- It is more efficient, especially with short locks.
- Method names became more intuitive: `EnterReadLock/ExitReadLock`, `EnterWriteLock/ExitWriteLock`, and `EnterUpgradeableReadLock/ ExitUpgradeableReadLock`.
- If we try to acquire a writer lock inside a reader lock, it will be an upgrade by default.
- Instead of using a timeout value, separate methods have been added: `TryEnterReadLock`, `TryEnterWriteLock`, and `TryEnterUpgradeableReadLock`, which make the code cleaner.

- Using nested locks is now forbidden by default. It is possible to allow nested locks by specifying a constructor parameter, but using nested locks is usually a mistake and this behavior helps to explicitly declare how it is intended to deal with them.

- Internal enhancements help to improve performance and avoid deadlocks.

The following is an example of different locking strategies for Dictionary<K,V> in the multiple readers / single writer scenario. First, we define how many readers and writers we're going to have, how long a read and write operation will take, and how many times to repeat those operations.

```
static class Program
{
  private const int _readersCount = 5;
  private const int _writersCount = 1;
  private const int _readPayload = 100;
  private const int _writePayload = 100;
  private const int _count = 100000;
```

Then we define the common test logic. The target dictionary is being created along with the reader and writer methods. The method called Measure uses LINQ to measure the performance of concurrent access.

```
private static readonly Dictionary<int, string> _map = new
    Dictionary<int, string>();

private static void ReaderProc()
{
  string val;
  _map.TryGetValue(Environment.TickCount % _count, out val);
  // Do some work
  Thread.SpinWait(_readPayload);
}

private static void WriterProc()
{
   var n = Environment.TickCount % _count;
   // Do some work
  Thread.SpinWait(_writePayload);
  _map[n] = n.ToString();
}

private static long Measure(Action reader, Action writer)
{
  var threads = Enumerable
      .Range(0, _readersCount)
      .Select(n => new Thread(
        () => {
```

```
                for (int i = 0; i < _count; i++)
                    reader();
            }))
        .Concat(Enumerable
            .Range(0, _writersCount)
            .Select(n => new Thread(
                () => {
                    for (int i = 0; i < _count; i++)
                        writer();
            })))
        .ToArray();
    _map.Clear();
    var sw = Stopwatch.StartNew();
    foreach (var thread in threads)
        thread.Start();

    foreach (var thread in threads)
        thread.Join();

    sw.Stop();
    return sw.ElapsedMilliseconds;
}
```

Then we use simple lock to synchronize concurrent access to the dictionary:

```
private static readonly object _simpleLockLock = new object();

private static void SimpleLockReader()
{
    lock (_simpleLockLock)
        ReaderProc();
}

private static void SimpleLockWriter()
{
    lock (_simpleLockLock)
        WriterProc();
}
```

The second test is using an older `ReaderWriterLock` class as follows:

```
private static readonly ReaderWriterLock _rwLock = new
    ReaderWriterLock();

private static void RWLockReader()
{
    _rwLock.AcquireReaderLock(-1);
    try
    {
        ReaderProc();
    }
```

```
      finally
      {
        _rwLock.ReleaseReaderLock();
      }
    }

    private static void RWLockWriter()
    {
      _rwLock.AcquireWriterLock(-1);
      try
      {
        WriterProc();
      }
      finally
      {
        _rwLock.ReleaseWriterLock();
      }
    }
```

Finally, we'll demonstrate the usage of ReaderWriterLockSlim:

```
    private static readonly ReaderWriterLockSlim _rwLockSlim = new
      ReaderWriterLockSlim();

    private static void RWLockSlimReader()
    {
      _rwLockSlim.EnterReadLock();
      try
      {
        ReaderProc();
      }
      finally
      {
        _rwLockSlim.ExitReadLock();
      }
    }

    private static void RWLockSlimWriter()
    {
      _rwLockSlim.EnterWriteLock();
      try
      {
        WriterProc();
      }
      finally
      {
        _rwLockSlim.ExitWriteLock();
      }
    }
```

Now we run all of these tests, using one iteration as a warm up to exclude any first run issues that could affect the overall performance:

```
static void Main()
{
  // Warm up
    Measure(SimpleLockReader, SimpleLockWriter);

    // Measure
    var simpleLockTime = Measure(SimpleLockReader,
      SimpleLockWriter);
    Console.WriteLine("Simple lock: {0}ms", simpleLockTime);

    // Warm up
    Measure(RWLockReader, RWLockWriter);

    // Measure
    var rwLockTime = Measure(RWLockReader, RWLockWriter);
    Console.WriteLine("ReaderWriterLock: {0}ms", rwLockTime);

    // Warm up
    Measure(RWLockSlimReader, RWLockSlimWriter);

     // Measure
    var rwLockSlimTime = Measure(RWLockSlimReader,
      RWLockSlimWriter);
    Console.WriteLine("ReaderWriterLockSlim: {0}ms",
      rwLockSlimTime);
  }
}
```

Executing this code on Core i7 2600K and x64 OS in the Release configuration gives the following results:

Simple lock: 367ms

ReaderWriterLock: 246ms

ReaderWriterLockSlim: 183ms

It shows that `ReaderWriterLockSlim` is about 2 times faster than the usual lock statement.

You can change the number of reader and writer threads, tweak the lock time, and see how the performance changes in each case.

Note that using a reader writer lock on the collection is not enough to provide a possibility to iterate over this collection. While the collection itself will be in the correct state, while iterating, if any of the collection items were removed or added, an exception will be thrown. This means, that you need to put all the iteration process inside a lock, or produce a new immutable copy of the collection and iterate over this copy.

Spin lock

Using operating system level synchronization primitives requires quite a noticeable amount of resources, because of the context switching and all the entire corresponding overhead. Besides this, there is such thing as lock latency; that is, the time required for a lock to be notified about the state change of another lock. This means that when the current lock is being released, it takes some additional time for another lock to be signaled. This is the reason why when we need short time locks, it could be significantly faster to use a single thread without any locks than to parallelize these operations using OS level locking mechanics.

To avoid unnecessary context switches in such a situation, we can use a loop, which checks the other locks in each iteration. Since the locks should be very short, we would not use too much CPU, and we have a significant performance boost by not using the operating system resources and by lowering lock latency to the lowest amount.

This pattern is not so easy to implement, and, to be effective, you would need to use specific CPU instructions. Fortunately, there is a standard implementation of this pattern in the .NET Framework starting with version 3.5. The implementation contains the following methods and classes:

Thread.SpinWait

`Thread.SpinWait` just spins an infinite loop. It's like `Thread.Sleep`, only without context switching and using CPU time. It is used rarely in common scenarios, but could be useful in some specific cases, such as simulating real CPU work.

System.Threading.SpinWait

`System.Threading.SpinWait` is a structure implementing a loop with a condition check. It is used internally in spinlock implementation.

System.Threading.SpinLock

Here we will be discussing about the spinlock implementation itself.

Note that it is a structure which allows to save on class instance allocation and reduces GC overhead.

The spinlock can optionally use a **memory barrier** (or a memory fencing instruction) to notify other threads that the lock has been released. The default behavior is to use a memory barrier, which prevents memory access operation reordering by compiler or hardware, and improves the fairness of the lock at the expense of performance. The other case is faster, but could lead to incorrect behavior in some situations.

Usually, it's not encouraged to use a spinlock directly unless you are 100% sure what you're doing. Make sure that you have confirmed the performance bottleneck with tests and you know that your locks are really short.

The code inside a spin lock **should not** do the following:

- Use regular locks, or a code that uses locks
- Acquire more than one spinlock at a time
- Perform dynamic dispatched calls (virtual methods, interface methods, or delegate calls)
- Call any third-party code, which is not controlled by you
- Perform memory allocation, including new operator usage

The following is a sample test for a spinlock:

```
static class Program
{
  private const int _count = 10000000;

  static void Main()
  {
    // Warm up
    var map = new Dictionary<double, double>();
    var r = Math.Sin(0.01);

    // lock
    map.Clear();
    var prm = 0d;
    var lockFlag = new object();
    var sw = Stopwatch.StartNew();
    for (int i = 0; i < _count; i++)
```

```
      lock (lockFlag)
      {
        map.Add(prm, Math.Sin(prm));
        prm += 0.01;
      }
    sw.Stop();
    Console.WriteLine("Lock: {0}ms", sw.ElapsedMilliseconds);

    // spinlock with memory barrier
    map.Clear();
    var spinLock = new SpinLock();
    prm = 0;
    sw = Stopwatch.StartNew();
    for (int i = 0; i < _count; i++)
    {
      var gotLock = false;
      try
      {
        spinLock.Enter(ref gotLock);
        map.Add(prm, Math.Sin(prm));
        prm += 0.01;
      }
      finally
      {
        if (gotLock)
          spinLock.Exit(true);
      }
    }
    sw.Stop();
    Console.WriteLine("Spinlock with memory barrier: {0}ms",
sw.ElapsedMilliseconds);

    // spinlock without memory barrier
    map.Clear();
    prm = 0;
    sw = Stopwatch.StartNew();
    for (int i = 0; i < _count; i++)
    {
      var gotLock = false;
      try
      {
        spinLock.Enter(ref gotLock);
        map.Add(prm, Math.Sin(prm));
        prm += 0.01;
```

```
      }
      finally
      {
        if (gotLock)
          spinLock.Exit(false);
      }
    }
    sw.Stop();
    Console.WriteLine("Spinlock without memory barrier: {0}ms",
  sw.ElapsedMilliseconds);
    }
}
```

Executing this code on Core i7 2600K and x64 OS in Release configuration gives the following results:

Lock: 1906ms

Spinlock with memory barrier: 1761ms

Spinlock without memory barrier: 1731ms

Note that the performance boost is very small even with short duration locks. Also note that starting from .NET Framework 3.5, the `Monitor`, `ReaderWriterLock`, and `ReaderWriterLockSlim` classes are implemented with spinlock.

The main disadvantage of spinlocks is intensive CPU usage. The endless loop consumes energy, while the blocked thread does not. However, now the standard `Monitor` class can use spinlock for a short time lock and then turn to usual lock, so in real world scenarios the difference would be even less noticeable than in this test.

Optimization strategy

Creating parallel algorithms is not a simple task: there is no universal solution to it. In every case, you have to use a specific approach to write effective code. However, there are several simple rules that work for most of the parallel programs.

Lock localization

The first thing to take into account when writing parallel code is to lock as little code as possible, and ensure that the code inside the lock runs as fast as possible. This makes it less deadlock-prone and scale better with the number of CPU cores. To sum up, acquire the lock as late as possible and release it as soon as possible.

Let us consider the following situation: for example, we have some calculation performed by method `Calc` without any side effects. We would like to call it with several different arguments and store the results in a list. The first intention is to write the code as follows:

```
for (var i = from; i < from + count; i++)
  lock (_result)
    _result.Add(Calc(i));
```

This code works, but we call the `Calc` method and perform the calculation inside our lock. This calculation does not have any side effects, and thus requires no locking, so it would be much more efficient to rewrite the code as shown next:

```
for (var i = from; i < from + count; i++)
{
  var calc = Calc(i);
  lock (_result)
    _result.Add(calc);
}
```

If the calculation takes a significant amount of time, then this improvement could make the code run several times faster.

Shared data minimization

Another way of improving parallel code performance is by minimizing the shared data, which is being written in parallel. It is a common situation when we lock over the whole collection every time we write into it, instead of thinking and lowering the amount of locks and the data being locked. Organizing concurrent access and data storage in a way that it minimizes the number of locks can lead to a significant performance increase.

In the previous example, we locked the entire collection each time, as described in the previous paragraph. However, we really don't care about which worker thread processes exactly what piece of information, so we could rewrite the previous code like the following:

```
var tempRes = new List<string>(count);
for (var i = from; i < from + count; i++)
{
  var calc = Calc(i);
  tempRes.Add(calc);
}
lock (_result)
  _result.AddRange(tempRes);
```

The following is the complete comparison:

```
static class Program
{
  private const int _count = 1000000;
  private const int _threadCount = 8;

  private static readonly List<string> _result = new
    List<string>();

  private static string Calc(int prm)
  {
    Thread.SpinWait(100);
    return prm.ToString();
  }

  private static void SimpleLock(int from, int count)
  {
    for (var i = from; i < from + count; i++)
      lock (_result)
      _result.Add(Calc(i));
  }

  private static void MinimizedLock(int from, int count)
  {
    for (var i = from; i < from + count; i++)
    {
      var calc = Calc(i);
      lock (_result)
      _result.Add(calc);
    }
  }

  private static void MinimizedSharedData(int from, int count)
  {
    var tempRes = new List<string>(count);
    for (var i = from; i < from + count; i++)
    {
      var calc = Calc(i);
      tempRes.Add(calc);
    }
    lock (_result)
      _result.AddRange(tempRes);
  }
```

```
private static long Measure(Func<int, ThreadStart> actionCreator)
{
  _result.Clear();
  var threads =
    Enumerable
      .Range(0, _threadCount)
      .Select(n => new Thread(actionCreator(n)))
      .ToArray();
  var sw = Stopwatch.StartNew();
  foreach (var thread in threads)
    thread.Start();
  foreach (var thread in threads)
    thread.Join();
  sw.Stop();
  return sw.ElapsedMilliseconds;
}

static void Main()
{
  // Warm up
  SimpleLock(1, 1);
  MinimizedLock(1, 1);
  MinimizedSharedData(1, 1);

  const int part = _count / _threadCount;

  var time = Measure(n => () => SimpleLock(n*part, part));
  Console.WriteLine("Simple lock: {0}ms", time);

  time = Measure(n => () => MinimizedLock(n * part, part));
  Console.WriteLine("Minimized lock: {0}ms", time);

  time = Measure(n => () => MinimizedSharedData(n * part, part));
  Console.WriteLine("Minimized shared data: {0}ms", time);
  }
}
```

Executing this code on Core i7 2600K and x64 OS in Release configuration gives the following results:

```
Simple lock: 806ms
Minimized lock: 321ms
Minimized shared data: 165ms
```

Summary

In this chapter, we learned about the issues with using shared data from multiple threads. We looked through the different techniques allowing us to organize concurrent access to shared state more efficiently in different scenarios. We also established an understanding about the performance issues of using locks, thread blocking, and context switching.

In the next chapter, we will continue to explore concurrent access to shared data. However, this time we will try to avoid locks and make our parallel program more robust and efficient.

2
Lock-Free Concurrency

In *Chapter 1, Traditional Concurrency*, we reviewed thread synchronization with locking and how to use locks effectively. However, there will be still performance overhead related to locking. The best way to avoid such issues is by not using locks at all whenever possible. Algorithms that do not use locking are referred to as **lock-free** algorithms.

Lock-free algorithms in turn are of different types. One of the most important types is **wait-free** algorithms. These algorithms not only evade the use of locks, but also are guaranteed to not wait for any events from other threads. This is a best-case scenario but unfortunately, it is a rare situation when we can avoid waiting for the other threads at all. Usually, a real concurrent program tries to be as close as possible to wait-free, and this is what every developer should try to achieve.

There is one more category of algorithms that do not use OS-level thread blocking but use spin locks. This allows the creation of quite efficient code in situations when the code inside the lock has to run very fast. Such algorithms can be called lock-free in various sources, but strictly speaking they are not as they do not guarantee that the algorithm will be progressing, since it is possible it gets blocked in various situations. We will discuss such situations later in *Chapter 10, Troubleshooting Parallel Programs*.

Please notice that a multithreaded program can be targeted in different scenarios, and thus the metrics could be different. For example, if our goal is to save the battery charge of a laptop or to save the CPU workload, locking techniques are preferred (until some point when there will be too many blocked threads). However, if we need overall performance, then lock-free algorithms are usually better.

Memory model and compiler optimizations

Memory model and compiler optimizations are not directly related to concurrency, but they are very important concepts for anyone who creates concurrent code, shown as follows:

```
class Program
{
  bool _loop = true;

  static void Main(string[] args)
  {
    var p = new Program();

    Task.Run(() =>
    {
      Thread.Sleep(100);
      p._loop = false;
    });

    while (p._loop);
    //while (p._loop) { Console.Write("."); };

    Console.WriteLine("Exited the loop");
  }
}
```

If you compile this with the Release build configuration and JIT compiler optimizations enabled, the loop will usually hang on the x86 and x64 architectures. This happens because JIT optimizes the p._loop read and does something like this:

```
if(p._loop)
{
  while(true);
}
```

If there is something inside the while loop, JIT will probably not optimize this code in this way. Also, we may use the **volatile** keyword with the Boolean flag like this:

```
volatile bool _loop;
```

In this case, JIT will turn off this optimization as well. This is where we use a memory model, and it gets complicated here. Here is a quote from the C# language specification:

> *For non-volatile fields, optimization techniques that reorder instructions can lead to unexpected and unpredictable results in multi-threaded programs that access fields without synchronization such as that provided by the lock-statement. These optimizations can be performed by the compiler, by the run-time system, or by hardware. For volatile fields, such reordering optimizations are restricted:*
>
> *•A read of a volatile field is called a volatile read. A volatile read has "acquire semantics"; that is, it is guaranteed to occur prior to any references to memory that occur after it in the instruction sequence.*
>
> *•A write of a volatile field is called a volatile write. A volatile write has "release semantics"; that is, it is guaranteed to happen after any memory references prior to the write instruction in the instruction sequence.*

As we can see, there is nothing specifically stated here about compiler optimizations, but in fact JIT does not optimize volatile field read in this case.

So we can see a description in a specification, but how does this really work? Let's look at a volatile read example:

```
class VolatileRead
{
  int _x;
  volatile int _y;
  int _z;

  void Read()
  {
    int x = _x; // 1
    int y = _y; // 2 (volatile)
    int z = _z; // 3
  }
}
```

The possible reordering options would be 1, 2, 3 (original); 2, 1, 3; and 2, 3, 1. This can be imagined as a one-way fence that allows the preceding operation to pass through, but does not allow subsequent operations. So this is called the **acquire fence**.

Volatile writes look pretty similar. Consider the following code snippet:

```
class VolatileWrite
{
  int _x;
  volatile int _y;
  int _z;

  void Read()
  {
    _x = 1; // 1
    _y = 2; // 2 (volatile)
    _z = 3; // 3
  }
}
```

Possible options here are 1, 2, 3 (original); 1, 3, 2; and 3, 1, 2. This is the **release fence**, which allows the reordering of only subsequent read or write operations but does not allow the preceding write operation. We have the `Thread.VolatileRead` and `Thread.VolatileWrite` methods that do the same thing explicitly. There is the `Thread.MemoryBarrier` (**memory barrier**) method as well, which allows us to use a full fence when we do not let through any operations.

I would like to mention that we are now on less certain ground. Different memory models on different architectures can be confusing, and code without **volatile** can perfectly work on x86 and amd64. However, if you are using shared data, please be aware of possible reordering and non-reordering optimizations and choose the appropriate behavior.

 Please be aware that making a field volatile means that all the read and write operations will have slightly lower performance and they will have the code in common, since some possible optimizations will be ignored.

The System.Threading.Interlocked class

When we reviewed race conditions in the previous chapter, we learned that even a simple increment operation consists of three separate actions. Although modern CPUs can perform such operations at once, it is necessary to make them safe to be used in concurrent programs.

The .NET Framework contains the `System.Threading.Interlocked` class that
provides access to several operations that are **atomic**, which means that they are
uninterruptible and appear to occur instantaneously to the rest of the system.
These are the operations that the lock-free algorithms are based on.

Let's revise a race condition example and compare the locking and `Interlocked`
class operations. First, we will use the traditional locking approach:

```
var counterLock = new object();
var counter = 0;
ThreadStart proc =
   () =>
   {
     for (int i = 0; i < count; i++)
     {
       lock (counterLock)
         counter++;
       Thread.SpinWait(100);
       lock (counterLock)
         counter--;
     }
   };
var threads =
   Enumerable
     .Range(0, 8)
     .Select(n => new Thread(proc))
     .ToArray();
var sw = Stopwatch.StartNew();
foreach (var thread in threads)
   thread.Start();
foreach (var thread in threads)
   thread.Join();
sw.Stop();
Console.WriteLine("Locks: counter={0}, time = {1}ms", counter,
   sw.ElapsedMilliseconds);
```

Now, let's replace locking with the `Interlocked` class method calls:

```
counter = 0;
ThreadStart proc2 =
   () =>
   {
     for (int i = 0; i < count; i++)
     {
       Interlocked.Increment(ref counter);
```

```
      Thread.SpinWait(100);
      Interlocked.Decrement(ref counter);
  }
};
threads =
  Enumerable
    .Range(0, 8)
    .Select(n => new Thread(proc2))
    .ToArray();
sw = Stopwatch.StartNew();
foreach (var thread in threads)
  thread.Start();
foreach (var thread in threads)
  thread.Join();
sw.Stop();
Console.WriteLine("Lock free: counter={0}, time = {1}ms", counter,
sw.ElapsedMilliseconds);
```

As a result, we got this on a reference computer:

```
Locks: counter=0, time = 1892ms
Locks: counter=0, time = 800ms
```

Just using atomic operations performed more than twice as well and kept the program logic correct.

Another tricky part is 64-bit integer calculations. When the program runs in the 64-bit mode, the read and write operations for 64-bit integer numbers are atomic. However, when running in the 32-bit mode, these operations become nonatomic and consist of two parts—reading/writing high 32 bits and low 32 bits of the number.

The Interlocked class contains the Read method that can read a 64-bit integer in the 32-bit mode as an atomic operation. This is not required in 64-bit mode, but if you compile your program in any CPU mode then you should use this method to guarantee atomicity of reads. There are the Increment and Decrement method overloads for 64-bit integers as well, and there is the Add method that allows us to have atomic addition of 32-bit and 64-bit integers.

Another very important operation is the value exchange. Looking at the following code it is obvious that this operation is not atomic, and thus we must put this code inside some kind of lock to keep this operation correct in a concurrent program:

```
var tmp = a;
a = b;
b = tmp;
```

The `Interlocked` class allows us to perform this operation as atomic with the `Exchange` method:

```
b = Interlocked.Exchange(ref a, b)
```

There are several overloads for this method that allow us to exchange the numeric values of different types including 32-bit and 64-bit integers, the `float` and `double` values, object references (there is a generic version of this method with the `type` parameter), and the `IntPtr` structures.

The most complicated atomic operation provided by the `Interlocked` class is the `CompareExchange` method. It accepts three arguments, then it compares the first argument with the third; if they are equal, it assigns the second argument value to the first argument. This is performed by special instruction on hardware too. We will see an example of this later in this chapter when we try to implement a lock-free queue.

[All the `Interlocked` class method calls implicitly generate full fences.]

Interlocked internals

To understand how interlocked internals work under the hood, we're going to see what machine code is being generated when compiling the `Interlocked.Increment` method. If we just run the program in debug mode and look at the disassembly window, we will see the usual method call.

To see what is really going on, we have to enable all optimizations:

1. First, we need to build the code in the Release mode in Visual Studio.

2. Then, we have to go to **Tools** | **Options** | **Debugging** | **General** and uncheck the **Suppress JIT optimization on module load** option.

3. Finally, add a `System.Diagnostics.Debugger.Break()` method call to pause the code in debugger.

If everything is set, you will see the following code in the disassembly window:

```
Interlocked.Increment(ref counter);

00007FFEF22B49AE   lea        rcx,[rsi+20h]
00007FFEF22B49B2   lock add   dword ptr [rcx],1
```

Please notice the **lock** prefix in the last line of the code. This prefix is an instruction to the CPU to perform an atomic increment operation. This means that the `Interlocked` class is not a usual class, but a hint to the JIT compiler to generate a special code.

Writing lock-free code

Since we have a very limited number of atomic operations, it is very hard to write lock-free code. For some common data structures, such as a double linked list, there is no lock-free implementation. Besides, it is very easy to make a mistake, and the main problem is that such code could work fine 99.9 percent of the time, which makes debugging enormously confusing.

Therefore, the best practice is to use standard implementations of such algorithms. A good place to start is by using concurrent collections from the `System. Collections.Concurrent` namespace that was introduced in the .NET Framework 4.0. We will review them in detail in *Chapter 6, Using Concurrent Data Structures*. However, now we will try to do not as advised and implement a lock-free stack and a lock-free queue from scratch.

The cornerstone of the lock-free code is the following pattern: read some data from the shared state, calculate a new value, and then write the new value back, but only if the shared state wasn't mutated by any other thread by that time. The last check and write operation must be atomic, and this is what we use `Interlocked. CompareExchange` for. This description looks a bit confusing, but it can be illustrated with quite an easy example. Imagine multiple threads calculating an integer sum in parallel. Consider the following line of code, for example:

```
_total += current;
```

If we use this simple code, we would get race condition here since this operation is not atomic. The easiest way to fix this is by using atomic addition with the `Interlocked.Add` method, but to illustrate the `CompareExchange` method logic, let's implement the addition like this:

```
int beforeValue, newValue;
do
{
  beforeValue = _total;
  newValue = beforeValue + current;
}
while (beforeValue != Interlocked.CompareExchange(ref _total,
  newValue, beforeValue))
```

First, we save the `_total` value in the `beforeValue` temporary variable. Then, we calculate a new value and store it in `newValue`. Finally, we're trying to save `newValue` in `_total`, but only if `_total` remains the same when we started the operation. If not, it means that the `_total` value has been changed by another thread and we have to repeat the operation with the new value of `_total`.

The ABA problem

Remember when we mentioned that lock-free programming is very complicated? Now, it's time to prove it. Here is another case when a seemingly right concurrent code works absolutely wrong.

Imagine that we have a lock-free stack implementation with the `Interlocked.CompareExchange` atomic **compare-and-swap (CAS)** operation. Let's assume that it contains three items: A on top, B, and C. Thread 1 calls the `Pop` method; it sets the old head value as A and the new head value as B. However for some reason, thread 1 gets suspended by the operating system. Meanwhile, thread 2 pops item A from the stack and saves it for later use. Then, it pushes item D on the stack. After doing this, it finally pushes item A back on top of the stack, but this time A's next item is D and our stack contains four items: A on top, D, B, and C.

Now the first thread continues to run. It compares whether the old head value and the current head value are the same, and they are! Therefore, the thread writes value B to the head of the stack. Now, the stack is corrupted and contains two items: B on the top and C.

The described process can be illustrated by the following schema:

Thread 1	Stack	Thread 2
1. Begins to pop an item from the stack. (head = A, new head = B)	A B C	
	B C	2. Pops an A from the stack. Stores A in variable.
	D B C	3. Pushes D on the stack.
	A D B C	4. Pushes A back on the stack.
Thread continues. CAS operation succeeds, since current head of the stack is A. New head is B, and the stack is corrupted	B C	

So, just having atomic CAS operations is not enough. To make this code work right, it's very important to make sure that we do not reuse references in our code or allow them to escape to our consumers. Thus, when we push item A twice, it should be different from the existing items from the stack perspective. To achieve this, it's enough to allocate a new wrapper object each time something is being pushed onto the stack.

Here is a quote from Wikipedia that describes the ABA problem very well:

> *Natalie is waiting in her car at a red traffic light with her children. Her children start fighting with each other while waiting, and she leans back to scold them. Once their fighting stops, Natalie checks the light again and notices that it's still red. However, while she was focusing on her children, the light had changed to green, and then back again. Natalie doesn't think the light ever changed, but the people waiting behind her are very mad and honking their horns now.*

The lock-free stack

Now, we are ready to implement a lock-free stack data structure. First, we define a base abstract class for our stack implementation:

```
public abstract class StackBase<T>
```

Then we have an inner class to define an item on the stack:

```
private class Item
{
  private readonly T _data;
  private readonly Item _next;

  public Item(T data, Item next)
  {
    _data = data;
    _next = next;
  }

  public T Data
  {
    get { return _data; }
  }

  public Item Next
  {
    get { return _next; }
  }
}
```

The item class contains user data and a reference to the next element on the stack. Now, we're adding a stack top item:

```
private Item _head;
```

A property that indicates whether the stack is empty is as follows:

```
public bool IsEmpty
{
  get { return _head == null; }
}
```

Two abstract methods that store and retrieve an item from the stack:

```
public abstract void Push(T data);

public abstract bool TryPop(out T data);
```

Now we have a base for different stack implementations to compare how they perform. We start with a lock-based stack:

```
public class LockStack<T> : StackBase<T>
```

As we remember, the lock statement is translated to the `Monitor` class method calls by the C# compiler. The monitor class tries to avoid using OS-level locks and uses spin locks to achieve a performance boost when a lock takes a little time. We're going to illustrate this and create a stack that uses only OS-level locks with the help of the `System.Threading.Mutex` class, which uses the **mutex** synchronization primitive from the OS. We create a mutex instance:

```
private readonly Mutex _lock = new Mutex();
```

Then, implement the `Push` and `Pop` methods as follows:

```
public override void Push(T data)
{
  _lock.WaitOne();
  try
  {
    _head = new Item(data, _head);
  }
  finally
  {
    _lock.ReleaseMutex();
  }
}


public override bool TryPop(out T data)
{
  _lock.WaitOne();
  try
  {
    if (IsEmpty)
    {
      data = null;
      return false;
    }
    data = _head.Data;
```

```
      _head = _head.Next;
      return true;
    }
    finally
    {
      _lock.ReleaseMutex();
    }
  }
```

This implementation puts a thread in a blocked state every time it has to wait for the lock to be released. This is the worst-case scenario, and we're going to see the test results that prove this.

Now we will implement a concurrent stack with a monitor and lock statement:

```
public class MonitorStack<T> : StackBase<T> where T: class
{
  private readonly object _lock = new object();

  public override void Push(T data)
  {
    lock (_lock)
      _head = new Item(data, _head);
  }

  public override bool TryPop(out T data)
  {
    lock (_lock)
    {
      if (IsEmpty)
      {
        data = null;
        return false;
      }
      data = _head.Data;
      _head = _head.Next;
      return true;
    }
  }
}
```

Then it's the lock-free stack implementation's turn:

```
public class LockFreeStack<T> where T: class
```

Notice that we had to add **class constraint** to the generic type parameter. We do this because we cannot atomically exchange values that are more than 8 bytes in size. If we look at the generic version of the `Interlocked.CompareExchange` method, we can make sure that its `type` parameter has the same class constraint.

Let's get to implementation:

```
public void Push(T data)
{
  Item item, oldHead;
  do
  {
    oldHead = _head;
    item = new Item(data, oldHead);
  } while (oldHead != Interlocked.CompareExchange(ref _head, item,
    oldHead));
}
```

This implementation is quite similar to a lock-free addition example. We basically do the same thing, only instead of addition, we're storing a new reference to the stack's head.

The `TryPop` method code is slightly more complicated:

```
public bool TryPop(out T data)
{
  var oldHead = _head;
  while (!IsEmpty)
  {
    if (oldHead == Interlocked.CompareExchange(ref _head,
      oldHead.Next, oldHead))
    {
      data = oldHead.Data;
      return true;
    }
    oldHead = _head;
  }
  data = null;
  return false;
}
```

Here we have to notice that the stack can be empty; in this case, we return `false` to indicate that we failed to retrieve a value from the stack.

Also, we would like to compare our code to the standard `ConcurrentStack` implementation from `System.Collections.Concurrent`. It is possible to use an interface to work with all collections in the same way, but in this case, it is easier to create a wrapper class that contains the source collection:

```
public class ConcurrentStackWrapper<T> : StackBase<T>
{
  private readonly ConcurrentStack<T> _stack;
  public ConcurrentStackWrapper()
  {
    _stack = new ConcurrentStack<T>();
  }

  public override void Push(T data)
  {
    _stack.Push(data);
  }

  public override bool TryPop(out T data)
  {
    return _stack.TryPop(out data);
  }
}
```

The only operation left is to compare the performances of our stack implementations:

```
private static long Measure(StackBase<string> stack)
{
  var threads = Enumerable
    .Range(0, _threadCount)
    .Select(
      n => new Thread(
        () =>
        {
          for (var j = 0; j < _iterations; j++)
          {
            for (var i = 0; i < _iterationDepth; i++)
            {
              stack.Push(i.ToString());
            }

            string res;

            for (var i = 0; i < _iterationDepth; i++)
            {
```

```
                    stack.TryPop(out res);
                }
            }
        }))
    .ToArray();
var sw = Stopwatch.StartNew();
foreach (var thread in threads)
    thread.Start();
foreach (var thread in threads)
    thread.Join();
sw.Stop();
if (!stack.IsEmpty)
    throw new ApplicationException("Stack must be empty!");
return sw.ElapsedMilliseconds;
}
```

We run several threads and each of these threads pushes and pops items to the stack in parallel. We wait for all the threads to complete, and check whether the stack is empty, which means that the program is correct. Finally, we measure the time required for all the operations to complete.

The results can be different and greatly depend on the CPU. This one is from a 3.4 GHz quad core Intel i7-3770 CPU:

LockStack: 6718ms

LockFreeStack: 209ms

MonitorStack: 154ms

ConcurrentStack: 121ms

This one is from a hyper-v virtual machine with two CPU cores running on a 2.2 GHz quad core Intel i7-4702HQ CPU laptop with power saving mode enabled:

LockStack: 39497ms

LockFreeStack: 388ms

MonitorStack: 691ms

ConcurrentStack: 419ms

The typical results are as follows: LockStack is the slowest, the LockFreeStack and MonitorStak implementations perform about the same, and the standard ConcurrentStack shows the best results. The MonitorStack implementation works well because, in this case, operations under lock are very fast, that is, about two processor cycles, and in this situation, spin wait works very well. We'll get back to explaining these results in detail later in *Chapter 6, Using Concurrent Data Structures*.

The lock-free queue

Stack and queue are the simplest of basic data structures. We have implemented a lock-free stack, and we encountered several tricky problems that we had to resolve. Implementing a lock-free concurrent queue is a more sophisticated task, since we now have to perform several operations at once. For example, when we queue a new item, we must simultaneously set the old tail's next item reference to a new item and then change a tail reference that the new item is now a new tail. Unfortunately, we cannot change two objects as an atomic operation. So, we must find a way to properly synchronize access to the head and tail without locks:

```
public class LockFreeQueue<T>
{
```

We define a simple class that is going to contain data in the queue:

```
protected class Item
{
  public T Data;
  public Item Next;
}
```

We will store references to the queue's tail and head and initialize them by default:

```
private Item _head;
private Item _tail;

public LockFreeQueue()
{
  _head = new Item();
  _tail = _head;
}
```

The first challenge is to implement an Enqueue method. What we can do is set tail. Next in the CAS operation, but let the tail reference advance later, maybe by other threads. This guarantees that the linked list of queue items will always be valid, and if we see that we failed to set a new tail, just let this operation start in another thread:

```
public void Enqueue(T data)
{
```

Create a new queue item and reserve space for the local copies of the `_tail` and `_tail.Next` references:

```
Item item = new Item();
item.Data = data;

Item oldTail = null;
Item oldNext = null;
```

We repeat the queueing operation until it succeeds:

```
bool update = false;
while (!update) {
```

Copy references to local variables and acquire a full fence so that the read and write operations will not be reordered. We have to use the `Next` field from the local copy, because the actual `_tail` item may have already been changed between both the read operations:

```
oldTail = _tail;
oldNext = oldTail.Next;

Thread.MemoryBarrier();
```

The tail may remain the same as it was in the beginning of the operation:

```
if (_tail == oldTail)
{
```

In this case, the next reference was null, which means that no one changed the tail since we copied it to `oldNext`:

```
if (oldNext == null)
{
```

Here we can try queueing an item, and this will be the success of the whole operation:

```
    update = Interlocked.CompareExchange(ref _tail.Next,
        item, null) == null;
}
else
{
```

If not, it means that another thread is queueing a new item right now, so we should try to set the tail reference to point to its next node:

```
        Interlocked.CompareExchange(ref _tail, oldNext, oldTail);
    }
  }
}
```

Here we have successfully inserted a new item to the end of the queue, and now we're trying to update the tail reference. However, if we fail it is okay, since another thread will eventually do this in its Enqueue method call:

```
    Interlocked.CompareExchange(ref _tail, item, oldTail);
}
```

The main goal of dequeueing properly is to correctly work in situations when we have not yet updated the tail reference:

```
public bool TryDequeue(out T result)
{
```

We will create a loop that finishes if there is nothing to dequeue or if we have dequeued an item successfully:

```
result = default(T);
Item oldNext = null;
bool advanced = false;
while (!advanced)
{
```

We will make local copies of variables that are needed:

```
Item oldHead = _head;
Item oldTail = _tail;
oldNext = oldHead.Next;
```

Then, we will acquire a full fence to prevent read and write reordering:

```
Thread.MemoryBarrier();
```

There might be a case when the head item has not been changed yet:

```
if (oldHead == _head)
{
```

Then, we will check whether the queue is empty:

```
if (oldHead == oldTail)
{
```

In this case, this should be `false`. If not, it means that we have a lagging tail and we need to update it:

```
if (oldNext != null)

{

  Interlocked.CompareExchange(ref _tail, oldNext, oldTail);
  continue;
}
```

If we are here, we have an empty queue:

```
  result = default(T);
  return false;
}
```

Now we will get the dequeueing item and try to advance the head reference:

```
    result = oldNext.Data;
    advanced = Interlocked.CompareExchange(
    ref _head, oldNext, oldHead) == oldHead;
  }
}
```

We will remove any references that can prevent the garbage collector from doing its job, and then we will exit:

```
    oldNext.Data = default(T);
    return true;
  }

  public bool IsEmpty
  {
    get
    {
      return _head == _tail;
    }
  }
}
```

Then we will write the following code to unify access to queues and compare different ways to synchronize access to the queue. To write general performance measurement code, we need to write an interface:

```
public interface IConcurrentQueue<T>
{
  void Enqueue(T data);
```

```
    bool TryDequeue(out T data);
    bool IsEmpty { get; }
}
```

Both `LockFreeQueue` and the standard `ConcurrentQueue` are already implementing this interface, and all we need to do is to create a wrapper class like this:

```
class LockFreeQueueWrapper<T> : LockFreeQueue<T>,
  IConcurrentQueue<T> {}

class ConcurrentQueueWrapper<T> : ConcurrentQueue<T>,
  IConcurrentQueue<T> {}
```

We need a more advanced wrapper in the case of a non-thread-safe Queue collection:

```
class QueueWrapper<T> : IConcurrentQueue<T>
{
  private readonly object _syncRoot = new object();
  private readonly Queue<T> _queue = new Queue<T>();

  public void Enqueue(T data)
  {
    lock(_syncRoot)
    _queue.Enqueue(data);
  }

  public bool TryDequeue(out T data)
  {
    if (_queue.Count > 0)
    {
      lock (_syncRoot)
      {
        if (_queue.Count > 0)
        {
          data = _queue.Dequeue();
          return true;
        }
      }
    }
    data = default(T);
    return false;
  }

  public bool IsEmpty
  {
    get { return _queue.Count == 0; }
  }
}
```

We have used a **double checked locking** pattern inside the `TryDequeue` method. At first glance, it seems that the first `if` statement is not doing anything useful, and we can just remove it. If you do an experiment and run the program without the first check, it will run about 50 times slower. The goal of the first check is to see whether the queue is empty so that a lock is not acquired; the lock and other threads are allowed to access the queue. Making a lock code minimal is very important, and it is illustrated here very well.

Now we need performance measurement. We can write a generalized code and provide our different queues in a similar way:

```
private static long Measure(IConcurrentQueue<string> queue)
{
  var threads = Enumerable
  .Range(0, _writeThreads)
  .Select(n => new Thread(() =>
  {
    for (int i = 0; i < _iterations; i++)
    {
      queue.Enqueue(i.ToString());
      Thread.SpinWait(100);
    }
  }))
  .Concat(new[]{new Thread(() =>
  {
    var left = _iterations*_writeThreads;
    while (left > 0)
    {
      string res;
      if (queue.TryDequeue(out res))
        left--;
    }
  })
  })
  .ToArray();
  var sw = Stopwatch.StartNew();
  foreach (var thread in threads)
    thread.Start();
  foreach (var thread in threads)
    thread.Join();
  sw.Stop();
  if (!queue.IsEmpty)
    throw new ApplicationException("Queue is not empty!");
  return sw.ElapsedMilliseconds;
}
```

The last thing that we need is just run the program and the results are going to be like this:

```
private const int _iterations = 1000000;
private const int _writeThreads = 8;

public static void Main()
{
  Console.WriteLine("Queue: {0}ms", Measure(new
    QueueWrapper<string>()));
  Console.WriteLine("LockFreeQueue: {0}ms", Measure(new
    LockFreeQueueWrapper<string>()));
  Console.WriteLine("ConcurrentQueue: {0}ms", Measure(new
    ConcurrentQueueWrapper<string>()));
}
```

The output is as follows:

Queue: 3453ms

LockFreeQueue: 1868ms

ConcurrentQueue: 1162ms

These results show that our lock-free queue has an advantage over straightforward locking, but the standard `ConcurrentQueue` performs better. It uses complicated ways of storing data—a linked list of array segments, which allows us to organize a more optimal process of storing and reading data.

Summary

In this chapter, we have learned how we can synchronize concurrent access to shared data without locking. We found out what a memory model and atomic operation are and how the .NET Framework allows programmers to use them in code. We have discussed the major problems related to lock-free programming and made sure that atomicity is necessary, but not enough to make the concurrent code work right. Also, we have implemented a lock-free stack and queue and illustrated the lock-free approach with concrete examples.

In the next chapter, we will combine approaches that we have learned so far and see how we can structure a concurrent program to lower the performance overhead and optimize it, depending on what exactly the program does.

3
Understanding Parallelism Granularity

One of the most essential tasks when writing parallel code is to divide your program into subsets that will run in parallel and communicate between each other. Sometimes the task naturally divides into separate pieces, but usually it is up to you to choose which parts to make parallel. Should we use a small number of large tasks, many small tasks, or maybe large and small tasks at the same time?

Theoretically speaking, it does not matter. In case of an ideal computational device, it would have no overhead for creating a worker thread and distributing work between any numbers of threads. However, on a real CPU, this performance overhead is significant and it is very important to take this into account. The right way to split your program into parallel parts is the key to writing effective and fast programs. In this chapter, we are going to review this problem in detail.

The number of threads

One of the easiest ways to split your program into a parallel executing part is using threads. However, what is a thread's cost for the operating system and CPU? What number of threads is optimal?

In Windows and in the 32-bit mode, the maximum number of threads in your process is restricted by the virtual address space available, which is two gigabytes. A thread stack's size is one megabyte, so we can have maximum 2,048 threads. In a 64-bit OS for a 32-bit process, it should be 4,096. However in practice, the address space will be fragmented and occupied by some other data, and there are other reasons why the maximum number of threads can be significantly different.

The best way to find out what's going on is to write a code that checks our assumptions. Here we will print the current size of a handle, giving us a way to detect whether we are in 32-bit or 64-bit mode. Then the code will start new threads until we get any exception, and it will print out the number of threads that we were able to start:

```
Console.WriteLine(IntPtr.Size);
var cnt = 0;

try
{
  for (var i = 0; i < int.MaxValue; i++)
  {
    new Thread(() => Thread.Sleep(Timeout.Infinite)).Start();
    cnt++;
  }
}
Catch
{
  Console.WriteLine(cnt);
}
```

In 32-bit mode on 64-bit Windows, results could be like this:

4

1522

When we switch to 64-bit mode, we will get the following:

8

71926

 Please be aware that if we run this in 64-bit mode, the program will exhaust system resources and might cause the OS to hang!

In 64-bit mode, we have no tight address space restrictions anymore, but there are other limited resources such as operating system handles, kernel memory space, and more. So, we do not know exactly how many threads we should be able to run. However, why are we getting 1,522 threads while we expected to get about 4,000 when we compiled our program in 32-bit mode?

There are two reasons behind this:

- The first reason is that when we run a 32-bit process on 64-bit Windows, a thread will have a 64-bit stack as well, and the actual stack allocation will be 1 MB + 256 KB of the 64-bit stack (or even 1 MB on the Windows versions prior to Windows Vista).

- The second reason is that our process is limited to 2 GB of the address space. If we want to use more, we have to specify a special flag, **IMAGE_FILE_ LARGE_ADDRESS_AWARE,** for our program, which is set using the **/ LARGEADDRESSAWARE** linker option. We cannot set this flag directly in Visual Studio, but we are able to use a tool called **EditBin.exe**, which is included in Visual Studio installation.

To use this tool, just open Visual Studio Developer Command Prompt and run the following command:

```
editbin /LARGEADDRESSAWARE path\to\your\program.exe
```

To switch off this flag, use this syntax:

```
editbin /LARGEADDRESSAWARE:NO path\to\your\program.exe
```

If you set this flag for the preceding program, you will see that we are able to create about 3,200 threads. Notice that we can use the so-called **4-gigabyte tuning** on 32-bit Windows, and using this along with the preceding option, we can get 3GB of memory for our 32-bit process, which should give us about 3,000 threads.

However, do we need to create that many threads? A thread is a quite expensive resource, and if more threads are created, more corresponding work has to be performed by the CPU. Besides this, modern desktop CPUs support only a few parallel threads—from 2 to 12 at the moment. CPUs on servers have more cores and can run more threads, but server-side concurrency is quite different and will be reviewed later in detail in *Chapter 8, Server-Side Asynchrony.* Therefore, creating more threads will not make a program effective, but instead it will make the program slower.

To prove this, we need to explore a more complicated program than just using Thread.SpinWait to simulate CPU load. We would like to see a real computational task that will involve every CPU's block working under heavy load. A task like this can be an implementation of a ray tracing algorithm to render several spheres. Here is a quote from Wikipedia:

> *In computer graphics, ray tracing is a technique for generating an image by tracing the path of light through pixels in an image plane and simulating the effects of its encounters with virtual objects.*

It is relatively easy to implement, and it can be easily scaled because the different parts of a scene have no shared data and can be rendered independently. The full code can be found in the code samples of this chapter. The actual rendering code is placed inside the RenderScene method. It accepts start and end column numbers and an array of pixel colors, which will contain the results of a rendering process.

In the beginning, we defined the algorithm parameters. In the sample code, we will use the image dimensions of 1920x1920 pixels:

```
private const int _width = 1920;
private const int _height = 1920;
```

This may not fit into your screen, and to avoid complexity, scrolling was not implemented here. So, if the resultant image is too large, you can simply lower its size. However, the measurements were taken for the initial image size.

To display the rendering results, we will call the ShowResult method. It creates System.Drawing.Bitmap with rendering results, creates the PictureBox control with this bitmap data, and shows it in Windows Forms Application:

```
private static void ShowResult(Color[,] data)
{
  var bitmap = new Bitmap(_width, _height,
    PixelFormat.Format32bppArgb);
  for (var i = 0; i < _width; i++)
    for (var j = 0; j < _height; j++)
      bitmap.SetPixel(i, j, data[i, j]);
  var pic = new PictureBox {
    Image = bitmap,
    Dock = DockStyle.Fill
  };

  var form = new Form {
    ClientSize = new Size(_width, _height)
  };

  form.KeyDown += (s, a) => form.Close();
  form.Controls.Add(pic);
  Application.Run(form);
}
```

Then, we can run this code like this:

```
var data = new Color[_width, _height];
RenderScene(data, 0, _width);
ShowResult(data);
```

To render the scene, there are two loops going through the X and Y coordinates. To make the rendering process parallel, we can use the X coordinate to split the calculations between worker threads, so each thread will render its own columns set. Then we will increase the worker threads number and repeat the process to measure performance:

```
for (var threadCnt = 1; threadCnt <= 32; threadCnt++)
{
  var part = _width/threadCnt;
  var threads = Enumerable.Range(0, threadCnt)    .Select(
    n => {
      var startCol = n*part;
      var endCol = n == threadCnt - 1
        ? _width - (threadCnt - 1) * part - 1
        : (n + 1) * part;

      return new Thread(() =>
        RenderScene(data, startCol, endCol));
    }).ToArray();

  var sw = Stopwatch.StartNew();

  foreach (var thread in threads)
    thread.Start();
  foreach (var thread in threads)
    thread.Join();

  sw.Stop();

  Console.WriteLine("{0} threads. Render time {1}ms",
    threadCnt, sw.ElapsedMilliseconds);
}
```

This is the rendering result:

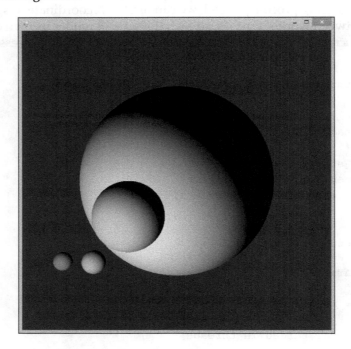

This is the dependency between the number of worker threads and the overall performance on a Core i7 2600K CPU and a 64-bit OS:

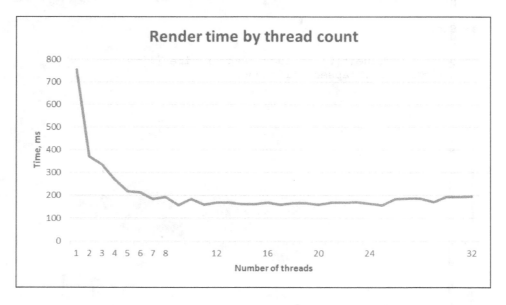

This chart shows three main stages. The first stage is a significant performance improvement when we increase the thread number up to four. An Intel Core i7 2600K CPU has four physical cores, and loading all the cores gives us almost linear scalability. Then we can have a smoother performance change while going from four to eight threads. This is due to the fact that this CPU supports **hyperthreading** technology. The hyper-threaded cores are implemented with a second set of hardware registers in the same core, but they use the same compute pipeline. Without going into too much detail, we can say that this often can be very efficient and can perform almost like two physical CPU cores. In this example, we can see that the hyperthreading technology allows the program to run faster.

The last stage is when we increase the threads number from 8 to 32. The line goes slightly up and this means that we do not gain any advantage and only lose performance. The CPU cannot perform faster because we have already put the maximum workload on it and creating more threads only leads to creating more work for running the threads and not calculations.

Thus, the most effective option is using as many threads as cores your CPU has and as many logical cores your operating system supports. 16 threads is a common number that will be enough for most of the present and near future desktop CPUs. The other option is to use the `Environment.ProcessorCount` variable to know during runtime how many cores the concrete CPU has.

Please notice that in general you should not use threads directly. There are other possibilities of running tasks in parallel, and you should use threads only when you are 100% aware of the advantages and disadvantages of other approaches. We'll review some of them later in this book.

Using the thread pool

As already mentioned, creating a thread is quite an expensive operation. In addition to this, creating more and more threads is not efficient. To make asynchronous operations easier, in Common Language Runtime there is a thread pool, which is represented by the `System.Threading.Threadpool` class. Instead of creating a thread every time we need one, we ask the thread pool for a worker thread. If it has a thread available, a thread pool returns it to us. When its job is done, it goes back into the thread pool in a suspended state until it is needed again.

There are two types of threads inside the thread pool: **worker threads** and **input/ output threads**. I/O threads are used for asynchronous I/O processing and we are not going to review them here. Let's concentrate on worker threads instead. This is what MSDN states about thread pool and its limits:

> *There is one thread pool per process.*
>
> *Beginning with the .NET Framework 4, the default size of the thread pool for a process depends on several factors, such as the size of the virtual address space. A process can call the GetMaxThreads method to determine the number of threads.*
>
> *The number of threads in the thread pool can be changed by using the SetMaxThreads method.*
>
> *Each thread uses the default stack size and runs at the default priority.*

If we try to acquire more worker threads than the thread pool's limit, the subsequent requests will be queued and will wait until a worker thread becomes available. So, we cannot have more thread pool worker threads than its limit at a time.

In practice, the thread pool implementation is very complicated and relies on empiric assumptions. Also, it has been changed with new .NET Framework versions, and it is possible that it will be changed in future, so we should not rely on specific implementation details.

However, the common logic is simple; the thread pool maintains a small number of worker threads and creates more threads when needed until the limit is reached. To see how this works, we can write a code that will create thread pool worker threads and see how many threads are being allocated at a time:

```
for (var i = 0; i < _threadCount; i++)
  ThreadPool.QueueUserWorkItem(
    s =>
    {
      Interlocked.Increment(ref _runCount);
      Thread.Sleep(5000);
      Interlocked.Decrement(ref _runCount);
    });
Thread.Sleep(1000);
while (_runCount > 0)
{
  Console.WriteLine(_runCount);
  Thread.Sleep(100);
}
```

We enqueue a number of worker threads, and each of them increments a thread counter, then waits for 5 seconds, and then decrements the counter, signaling that its work is finished. In the main thread, we print out this counter to see how the worker threads are being allocated.

For the .NET Framework 4.5 and a specific hardware, this code shows that at first we almost immediately have nine worker threads, then the counter grows slowly until 35-40, and then it goes back to 0. Thus, using the thread pool with a large number of tasks allows us to effectively load the CPU and abstract from the actual threads usage specifics.

There is one more worthwhile thing to mention about the thread pool that can be good or bad in different scenarios. There is one thread pool per process, and every library and framework that you use can potentially work with the thread pool, so some of the worker threads can be already busy with third-party code tasks. So, if some library is not well written and occupies many worker threads or blocks them with long-running operations, then your program will not be able to effectively load the CPU. Also, this can be caused by a third- party code that works with input/ output operation incorrectly, which leads to performance degradation as well.

So if your program uses the thread pool for computation tasks and the CPU is not fully loaded, it is worth checking how many worker threads are there and what exactly they are doing. Specifically, this is extremely important for server-side concurrency, where server frameworks usually share the thread pool with your code.

Understanding granularity

When there is one common computational task inside your application, it is quite obvious how to make it run in parallel. The most effective solution would be to divide the tasks in parts and run these parts on each available CPU core. Since the number of parts will not be large, there will not be any significant performance overhead. This way of dividing your code into parallel running tasks is called **coarse-grained**:

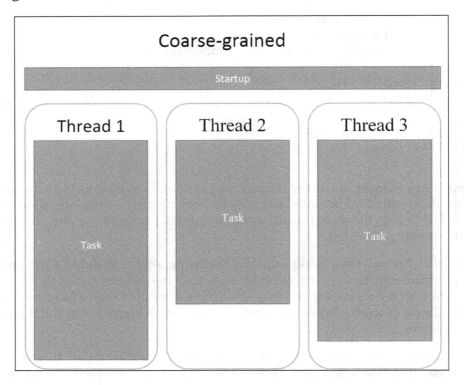

There is one problem with the coarse-grained approach. The large tasks can run at significantly different times, and then at these times, some of the CPU cores will not be used to help compute the other tasks. One more possibility is that these tasks can block the CPU cores while waiting for some signals from other threads or input/output operation to complete. In this case, the CPU time would be wasted.

To be more effective, we will have to split these tasks into more parts. If the number of parts will be less, then we will still have the problem of some tasks running much faster than others do and some of CPU cores will be unavailable for further computations. So, we have to split the tasks into many small pieces until we can say that blocking one task is not important because the CPU can switch to another task at once. This approach is called **fine-grained**:

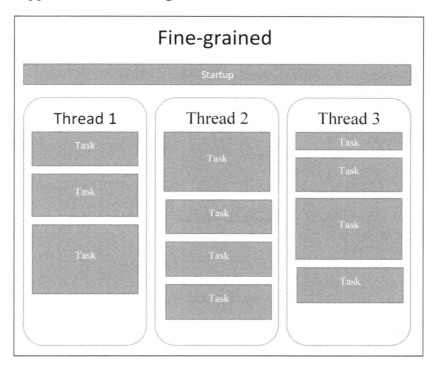

How can we implement such a program? We have to divide our computation into very small tasks and minimize the overhead for each task since there will be many of them, and we do not want to waste CPU time to support these tasks' infrastructure instead of doing computation. Then we have to find a way to run these tasks effectively.

It is very complicated to write a general algorithm to divide many different computation tasks into several worker threads. Fortunately, such frameworks already exist and one of them is included in the .NET Framework. It is called **Task Parallel Library** (TPL). We will discuss TPL in detail in *Chapter 4, Task Parallel Library in Depth*.

Now, we will use TPL to write a fine-grained parallel program. We simulate that the tasks are different by running SpinWait with different number of cycles. Then we split our tasks into differently-sized pieces and calculate the number of iterations per millisecond that we were able to run.

The sample code will be as follows:

```
var random = new Random();
var taskSizes =
  Enumerable
    .Range(0, _totalSize)
    .Select(n => random.NextDouble())
    .ToArray();
for (var workSize = 256; workSize > 0; workSize -= 4)
{
  var total = 0;
  var tasks = new List<Task>();
  var i = 0;
  while (total < _totalSize)
  {
    var currentSize = (int)(taskSizes[i]*workSize) + 1;
    tasks.Add(
      new Task(
        () =>
        {
          Thread.SpinWait(currentSize*_sizeElementaryDelay);
        }));
    i++;
    total += currentSize;
  }
  var sw = Stopwatch.StartNew();
  foreach (var task in tasks)
    task.Start();
  Task.WaitAll(tasks.ToArray());
  sw.Stop();
  Console.WriteLine(
    "Work size {0},
    Task count {1}, Effectiveness {2:####} works/ms",
    workSize, tasks.Count,
    ((double)total * _sizeElementaryDelay)/sw.ElapsedMilliseconds);
}
}
```

The fundamental entity in TPL is the `System.Threading.Task` class, which represents a basic task that has to be run. To compare the performance of large tasks versus small tasks, we will go through the following process:

- We prepare an array of random task sizes to create a unique set of tasks for each time we run the program.

- Then we split the total work into a small number of large tasks, run the measurement, and then repeat the whole process once again by splitting the work into smaller tasks and making the total number of tasks larger.

- Each measurement involves starting `Stopwatch`, running all tasks, waiting for all the tasks to complete with the `Task.WaitAll` method, and then measuring how much time it took to complete all the tasks.

Here is sample chart illustrating the results of running this code:

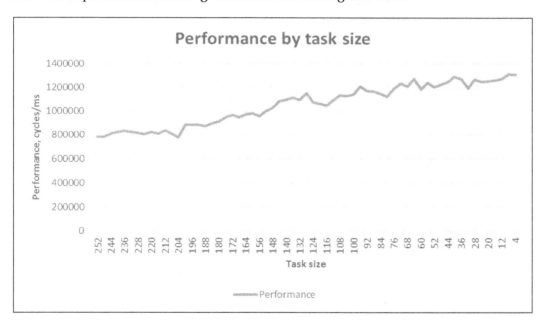

This chart shows that when we reduce task size, we increase performance until some point. Then the task size becomes small enough to achieve full CPU workload. Making tasks smaller becomes ineffective due to an overall task overhead increase.

This was a synthetic test. In practice, everything will depend on a program's nature. If it is possible to vary the task size for your program, and if performance is crucial, you can run several tests and find out the best parameters experimentally.

Choosing the coarse-grained or fine-grained approach

Fine-grained parallelism granularity allows us to run heterogeneous computational tasks effectively. Besides this, the fine-grained approach makes the splitting of your program into tasks easier, especially if these tasks are related to each other and, for example, latter tasks use some computation results of former tasks. However, we will have to trade off some performance, since the CPU has to be used to manage all these tasks as well.

To find out how fine-grained granularity can affect performance for a real task, let's implement a ray tracing algorithm using TPL and compare it to the results that we got in the beginning using an optimal number of threads. To implement the fine-grained program version, we will just create a task for each image column and start it immediately. The implementation code is as follows:

```
var tasks = new List<Task>();
var fineSw = Stopwatch.StartNew();
for (var i = 0; i < _width; i++)
{
  var col = i; // Create separate variable for closure
  tasks.Add(Task.Factory.StartNew(() => RenderScene(data, col,
    col)));
}
Task.WaitAll(tasks.ToArray());
fineSw.Stop();
Console.WriteLine("Fine grained {0}ms",
  fineSw.ElapsedMilliseconds);
```

Executing this code in coarse-grained mode takes about 150 milliseconds on the specific hardware. A fine-grained mode takes about 160 milliseconds. At first glance, the difference is insignificant. However, it is still noticeable, even after knowing that the TPL code is very well optimized. So, if performance is very important, it is possible to try implementing parallelism granularity by yourself. However before this, you must be absolutely sure that the bottleneck is granularity and the results of the tests conducted approve this.

If not, just use TPL and fine-grained approach, which is easy to code and still provides good performance.

Summary

In this chapter, we have reviewed a problem of parallel computations granularity. We have tried different ways to split our program into concurrently executing pieces and saw the performance impact in each case. Also, we've implemented a real computation task of rendering spheres with a ray tracing algorithm and learned to parallelize it with threads and Task Parallel Library.

In the next chapter, we will continue to learn Task Parallel Library. We shall review this framework in detail and clarify every aspect of using it including how the tasks are being run, how we combine tasks together, and how to handle exceptions and timeouts.

Task Parallel Library in Depth

In the previous chapter, we have already used TPL to simplify the writing of some fine-grained parallel code. The code looked quite clear; however, TPL is a quite complicated framework with a high level of abstraction, and it deserves a detailed review.

Most code samples that we have seen so far were quite simple in terms of composition. We took a computational problem, split it into several independent parts, and ran these parts on different worker threads. When all the parts are completed, we get their results and combine them into a final calculation result. However, most real-world programs usually have a complex structure. We need to get input data, and then there are program stages that depend on each other; to continue the calculations, we have to get results from previous stages. These stages can take different durations to complete and require different approaches for parallelization.

It is possible to write this logic based on worker threads and synchronization primitives. However, with many parts and dependencies, such code will become too large and verbose. To make the programming easier, we can take advantage of different **parallel programming model** implementations that abstract threads and synchronization mechanics and offer some kind of a higher-level API that is much easier to use. This is the parallel programming model definition from Wikipedia:

> *In computer software, a parallel programming model is a model for writing parallel programs which can be compiled and executed. The value of a programming model can be judged on its generality: how well a range of different problems can be expressed for a variety of different architectures, and its performance: how efficiently they execute. The implementation of a programming model can take several forms such as libraries invoked from traditional sequential languages, language extensions, or complete new execution models.*

One such model is **task-based parallelism**. Its main concept is a task, which is just a piece of synchronously executing code. If one task depends on another task's result, we can provide such information to the framework. The final part is the **task scheduler**. It knows about the current environment and can execute tasks on an optimal number of threads, taking into account the information about dependencies between the tasks. The program code transforms into defining tasks and their dependencies, which is much cleaner than raw threads or thread pool usage.

Let us reconsider a code sample from the previous chapter:

```
for (var i = 0; i < _width; i++)
{
  var col = i; // Create separate variable for closure
  tasks.Add(Task.Factory.StartNew(() => RenderScene(data, col,
    col)));
}
Task.WaitAll(tasks.ToArray());
```

Here, we have used a loop to iterate through all the columns of our scene, and then we split calculations to create a separate task for each column. To create such tasks, we use the `System.Threading.Task` class. The `StartNew` method creates a new `Task` instance and starts the task at once. When we have completed creating all the tasks, we will use the `Task.WaitAll` static method to wait until all the tasks complete their jobs.

Task composition

Let's consider a situation where, before running a task (let's call the task, task B), we will need a result from the calculation of a previous task, task A. Such dependency between tasks is usually called **future** or **promise**. This means that, when we run task A, we do not know its result before the calculations are complete. So we state (make a promise) that, at some point in the future, we will run task B as soon as we get the result from task A.

Why do we need to declare dependencies in a specific way? We can always create dependent tasks as follows:

```
var taskA = new Task<string>(
  () =>
  {
    Console.WriteLine("Task A started");
    Thread.Sleep(1000);
    Console.WriteLine("Task A complete");
    return "A";
  });
taskA.Start();
```

```
var taskB = new Task(
  () =>
  {
    Console.WriteLine("Task B started");
    Console.WriteLine("Task A result is {0}", taskA.Result);
  });
taskB.Start();
taskB.Wait();
```

The result is this:

Task A started

Task B started

Task A complete

Task A result is A

First, we create a new task A instance and use a thread pool worker thread to execute the code inside this task.

> By default, Task Parallel Library uses .NET as the thread pool to run task code. However, it is possible to use other ways to run tasks, and the part of TPL that is responsible for running tasks is called the **task scheduler**. We will review task schedulers later in this chapter.

The output displays **Task A started** and simulates some calculations using the Thread.Sleep method. At the same time, we will create a new task B instance, which uses another thread pool worker thread to run. It outputs **Task B started** to the console and then blocks until task A completes. Then, task A signals its completion by printing **Task A complete** and returns the "A" string as a result. Task B gets a signal that task A is completed and prints the result as **Task A result is A**.

So, it seems that we have successfully created two dependent tasks. Unfortunately, this code will be quite ineffective and hard to maintain. Imagine that we need more dependencies. This code will in turn create many tasks that will use other tasks' results, and to understand dependencies, a reader will have to analyze each task's code. Besides this, when task A runs, task B blocks the thread pool thread. It means that we have just wasted one worker thread that is doing nothing and cannot be used to serve some other job. If we create many tasks, we will soon take over all the worker threads from a thread pool, and this is a very bad practice that leads to scalability and performance problems.

Nevertheless, it is obvious that there is no sense in running tasks A and B in parallel, since B needs A to complete. To run this code synchronously, we can merge the code from A and B, but this would break up program logic and lead us back to the coarse-grained approach.

Another way is to analyze dependencies between tasks and use thread pool worker threads more efficiently. For example, do not schedule task B code execution until task A code finishes and returns its result. All we need to do is to declare a dependency between tasks explicitly, so TPL will know what tasks to run first and what to delay. This is exactly what the Task.ContiueWith method does. We use this method on an initial task, and this returns another task (usually called a **continuation task**) that will be executed after the former task completes:

```
var taskA = new Task<string>(
    () =>
    {
        Console.WriteLine("Task A started");
        Thread.Sleep(1000);
        Console.WriteLine("Task A complete");
        return "A";
    });
taskA
    .ContinueWith(
        task =>
        {
            Console.WriteLine("Task B started");
            Console.WriteLine("Task A result is {0}", task.Result);
        });
taskA.Start();
taskA.Wait();
```

We created a task A instance similar to the previous example. However, instead of creating a new task, we used the ContinueWith method on the task A instance that allows us to provide a code that will be run when task A completes. We have access to the task A instance via the task parameter of the lambda expression. Now the TPL task scheduler will place a continuation task code on a thread pool only after task A runs to completion.

The result of this code will be as follows:

Task A started

Task A complete

Task B started

Task A result is A

Notice that the order of messages is different than the previous result. Now task B is started after task A completes.

This can be a disadvantage if the latter task performs some work that can be run in parallel. In this case, running task B after A will be inefficient, since it is actually a synchronous code execution. However, TPL is about task composition and it simply means that we can split task B into two tasks; one will run in parallel with task A and the other will be placed in a continuation task:

```
var taskA = new Task<string>(
  () =>
  {
    Console.WriteLine("Task A started");
    Thread.Sleep(1000);
    Console.WriteLine("Task A complete");
    return "A";
  });
taskA.Start();

var taskB1 = new Task(() => Console.WriteLine("Task B1 started"));
taskB1.Start();

taskA.ContinueWith(tsk => Console.WriteLine("Task A result is
  {0}", tsk.Result));

taskA.Wait();
```

If we run this code, the results will show that task A and B1 run in parallel; B1 can even be run before A, since it does not really matter in terms of program logic in what order independent tasks are scheduled to run.

There are more complicated ways of composing tasks. For example, when a task needs results from multiple tasks, the ContinueWith method allows us to follow only one task, and we need task B2 to get the results from A and B1:

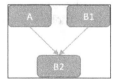

However, there is a TaskFactory class that can be accessed through the Task. Factory static property. It contains many useful things to create and schedule tasks, but what we need now is its ContinueWhenAll method.

The implementation of the multiple dependency schema is as follows:

```
var taskA = new Task<string>(
  () =>
  {
    Console.WriteLine("Task A started");
    Thread.Sleep(1000);
    Console.WriteLine("Task A complete");
    return "A";
  });
taskA.Start();

var taskB1 = new Task<string>(
  () =>
  {
    Console.WriteLine("Task B1 started");
    Thread.Sleep(500);
    Console.WriteLine("Task B1 complete");
    return "B";
  });
taskB1.Start();

Task
  .Factory
  .ContinueWhenAll(
    new []{taskA, taskB1},
    tasks => Console.WriteLine("Task A result is {0}, Task B
      result is {1}", tasks[0].Result, tasks[1].Result));

taskA.Wait();
```

The `ContinueWhenAll` method accepts an array of tasks as its first parameter and a lambda expression as the second. The lambda expression `tasks` parameter is the tasks array that we have just provided. Instead of using this, it is possible to create a closure and access the `taskB1` and `taskA` variables in the lambda body, but this would create unnecessary dependencies in the code, which is generally a bad practice.

> This is often referred to as **code coupling**. When the code has many dependencies, it is called **high coupling**; in this case, the code is hard to maintain, since any change can affect the other parts. **Low coupling** means that this part of the code does not depend on other parts, so it can be changed and maintained easily without breaking the other code, and other changes will most likely not break this part of the program.

The results will be as follows:

```
Task A started
Task B1 started
Task B1 complete
Task A complete
Task A result is A, Task B result is B
```

This shows that tasks A and B1 run independently in parallel, and the final code gets the results from both the tasks. We successfully described dependencies in a declarative way, and the TPL infrastructure ensured the correctness of the execution order and program logic.

It is worth mentioning another `TaskFactory` class method, the `ContinueWhenAny` method, which is quite similar to `ContinueWhenAll`. It creates a task that starts when any of the provided tasks in the array complete. This is useful for having several alternative ways to achieve the result, and we use the one that completes faster than the others.

Tasks hierarchy

We mentioned before that the task scheduler needs explicitly defined dependencies between tasks to run them effectively and in the correct order. However, besides this, there is a way to achieve implicit dependency definition; when we create one task inside another, a special parent-child dependency is created for these tasks. By default, this does not affect how these tasks will be executed, but there is a way to make this dependency really important.

We can create a task with the `TaskFactory.CreateNew` method by providing a special `TaskCreationOptions.AttachedToParent` parameter. This changes the usual task behavior, and the important differences are as follows:

- The parent task will not complete until every child task completes.
- If the case child tasks cause any exceptions, they will be translated to the parent task.
- The parent task status depends on its child tasks. If any child task fails, the parent task will have the `TaskStatus.Faulted` status as well.

To illustrate this, we can compare the behavior of the default task and the task attached to the parent. Here, we will create a child task without specifying the task creation options:

```
Task
  .Factory
  .StartNew(
    () =>
    {
      Console.WriteLine("Parent started");
      Task
        .Factory
        .StartNew(
          () =>
          {
            Console.WriteLine("Child started");
            Thread.Sleep(100);
            Console.WriteLine("Child complete");
          });
    })
  .Wait();
Console.WriteLine("Parent complete");
```

As a result we get the following:

Parent started

Child started

Parent complete

It is important that the parent task has completed before the child task, and since we waited only for the parent task, the main thread exited and the child task did not complete at all.

Now we add the `AttachedToParent` option in the same code, changing only the child task as follows:

```
Task
  .Factory
  .StartNew(
    () =>
    {
      Console.WriteLine("Child started");
      Thread.Sleep(100);
      Console.WriteLine("Child complete");
    },
    TaskCreationOptions.AttachedToParent);
```

Run this again to get the following:

```
Parent started
Child started
Child complete
Parent complete
```

Here, we can see that the parent task waits until the child task finishes and only then changes its status to `TaskStatus.RanToCompletion`.

Awaiting task completion

There are different ways to wait until the TPL task completes. In the previous code, we used the `Task.Wait` method. This method blocks the current thread until this task completes. If the task gives a result, the same effect can be achieved when the `Task.Result` instance property is queried. This is a basic way to coordinate tasks in the program.

When we needed to wait for multiple tasks, we used the `Task.WaitAll` static method. If we keep aside the optimization and exception handling code, this method will be implemented using the following logic:

```
var waitedOnTaskList = new List<Task>(tasks.Length);
for (int i = tasks.Length - 1; i >= 0; i--)
{
  Task task = tasks[i];
  if (!taskIsCompleted)
    waitedOnTaskList.Add(task);
}

if (waitedOnTaskList != null)
{
  WaitHandle[] waitHandles = new
    WaitHandle[waitedOnTaskList.Count];
  for (var i = 0; i < waitHandles.Length; i++)
    waitHandles[i] =
      waitedOnTaskList[i].CompletedEvent.WaitHandle;
  WaitAll(waitHandles);
}
```

We have defined a list of tasks that are not completed yet and then attached an array of handles to the OS-specific objects that can be used to wait for each task to be completed. Then we wait on these objects until all underlying tasks are completed.

As in the previous case, along with `WaitAll`, the `Task` type defines the `WaitAny` static method. It waits until any task in the array is completed. It can be used to track the progress of task completion or to choose the fastest way to get results from the several alternatives.

Task cancellation

A task represents a common asynchronous operation. This means that we don't know when it completes. Sometimes, it is clear that we do not need this task anymore. For example, if the operation takes too long to complete, or the user clicks on the **Cancel** button. In this case, we need to stop the task.

One of the lower-level ways to stop a thread is by calling its `Abort` method. Before going on, I would like to emphasize the importance of not using this.

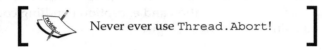 Never ever use `Thread.Abort`!

`Thread.Abort` raises a very special exception called `ThreadAbortException` on a thread that is being aborted. This exception can happen at more or less any point in your program and cannot be stopped by the usual exception handling. We can write a code with catch block and the code inside this block will work, but as soon as the catch block ends, the same exception will be raised again. But—surprise—if we call the `Thread.CurrentThread.ResetAbort` method inside the catch block, the thread abort request will be canceled. This means that calling `Thread.Abort` does not guarantee that the thread will be actually aborted.

Another aspect of using this method is that it affects only the managed code. If your thread is waiting for unmanaged code to complete, which is almost every I/O operation, the thread will not be aborted until this operation ends. If the operation never completes, the code will never return and your program will hang.

Also, due to the .NET CLR constructing type algorithm specifics, this exception can break your program. If there is an exception inside a static constructor of some type, this exception gets cached, and all further attempts to use this type will lead to throwing this exception. So if we call `Thread.Abort` and raise this exception while the target thread was executing any static constructor, we will get `ThreadAbortException` when any thread tries to access the type that failed to be created on the previous thread.

If this is not enough, there is one more illustration of how evil this exception is. Imagine the code that is usually written for working with files:

```
using (FileStream fs = File.Open(fileName, ...))
{
  ...do stuff with data file...
}
```

The preceding code is the shorter version of the following code:

```
FileStream fs = File.Open(fileName, ...);
try
{
  ...do stuff with data file...
}
finally
{
  IDisposable disposable = fs;
  disposable.Dispose();
}
```

Since `ThreadAbortException` can emerge at any point, it can happen inside the finally block. If it happens there, the code in this block will not run to completion and the file will remain opened. In this case, the `FileStream` class implements a disposable pattern and is likely to be closed while its finalizer method is called when garbage collection occurs. However, it is clear that leaving the file open for an undefined time is not a good thing and other code is not always correctly written.

Therefore, `Thread.Abort` must be avoided in all circumstances. Instead of using this, we should write the code while being aware of the cancellation possibility. It is important that this cancellation must not depend on any concrete ways of running the operation itself, since TPL abstracts away task execution mechanics, allowing us to write custom task schedulers and use them with standard TPL code.

Fortunately, the .NET Framework contains a Cancellation API, and this is what we should use to implement cancellation in our code. TPL uses this API as well, which makes it easier to write cancellation code for TPL-based programs.

The Cancellation API is based on two main types—the `System. Threading.CancellationToken` structure and the `System.Threading. CancellationTokenSource` class. The cancellation token contains methods and properties that we can use to handle the cancellation request, and the cancellation token source allows us to create cancellation tokens and initiate cancellation requests.

A typical situation is when we have two parts of a code. The first part is the code that creates, combines, and runs tasks. This code can interact with the program UI and handles situations when we need to cancel some of the running tasks. Usually, this part is responsible for creating `CancellationTokenSource`, constructing cancellation token instances, and providing them to each task that can be cancelled. Then, when the cancellation process is being initiated, we call the `Cancel` or `CancelAfter` methods on each cancellation token needed.

The second part of code lives inside tasks and uses cancellation token instances to get cancellation signals. There are several common approaches to implementing the cancellation itself. They are covered in the following sections.

Checking a flag

If the code inside a task is quite easy, for example, it is a loop with short iterations, then the easiest way to stop the operation is to check some flag variable inside this loop and exit if the flag is set.

The first part of the code creates a task, provides it with a cancellation token, and then initiates a cancellation process. Finally, we measure the time of the task cancellation process as follows:

```
private static void RunTest(Action<CancellationToken> action,
    string name)
{
    var cancelSource = new CancellationTokenSource();
    var cancelToken = cancelSource.Token;
    var task = Task
        .Factory
        .StartNew(() => action(cancelToken), cancelToken);

    // Wait for starting task
    while (task.Status != TaskStatus.Running) { }

    var sw = Stopwatch.StartNew();
    cancelSource.Cancel();
    while (!task.IsCompleted) {}
    sw.Stop();
    Console.WriteLine("{0} task cancelled in {1} ms", name,
        sw.ElapsedMilliseconds);
}
```

Notice that we are providing a cancellation token not only to our task, but also to the StartNew method as well. The reason for this is that TPL is aware of cancellation tokens as well and can cancel the task even if it has not started yet and our code is not able to handle cancellation.

Also, we use a loop instead of calling the Wait method. The Wait method has an overload accepting the cancellation token instance. If we call the Cancel method from the token, the Wait method will return the execution at once. This is a built-in cancellation mechanism in TPL, but we need custom cancellation now, so we emulate waiting with task status checking inside the loop. First, we wait until the task actually starts, and then we initiate cancellation and wait until the task completes.

Finally, we stop the timer and print out the results.

The code for the task runs an infinite loop, waits, and checks whether a cancellation is requested:

```
RunTest(tok =>
{
  while (true)
  {
    Thread.Sleep(100);
    if (tok.IsCancellationRequested)
      break;
  }
}, "CheckFlag");
```

The result can be like this:

CheckFlag task got cancelled in 103 ms

This means that the cancellation happened in the first loop iteration as soon as the task code checked the flag.

Throwing an exception

If the code inside the task is complicated, it is difficult to check the flag in every part of the code. There can be many loops inside many methods, and if we get results from a method that can be cancelled, we need to provide additional information to distinguish whether this method was cancelled or successfully ran to completion. In this case, it is much easier to use another cancellation technique—throwing a special cancellation exception.

If we use the `CancellationToken.ThrowIfCancellationRequested` method on our token, then it will throw `OperationCanceledException` when cancellation is requested. This exception will stop code execution inside the task, bubble up to the TPL infrastructure that will handle it, and set task status to `TaskState.Canceled`.

Instead of checking the flag, we instruct the token to raise `OperationCanceledException` when receiving a cancellation request:

```
RunTest( tok =>
{
  while (true)
  {
    Thread.Sleep(100);
    tok.ThrowIfCancellationRequested();
  }
}, "ThrowException");
```

The changes are minimal, and the result should be the same:

ThrowException task got cancelled in 109 ms

As soon as we get to the `ThrowIfCancellationRequested` method, the call operation gets cancelled with an exception.

Using OS wait objects with WaitHandle

The next option is useful when the code inside a task is waiting on an OS synchronization primitive for a significant time. Here, we can use `CancellationToken.WaitHandle` to include in the waiting process and react immediately when cancellation is requested.

This is usually combined with one of the previously described techniques — we just stop waiting and proceed with the cancellation.

This is how it looks:

```
RunTest(tok =>
{
  var evt = new ManualResetEvent(false);
  while (true)
  {
    WaitHandle.WaitAny(new[] { evt, tok.WaitHandle }, 100);
    tok.ThrowIfCancellationRequested();
  }
}, "WaitHandle");
```

In this example, we have created a `ManualResetEvent` instance to wait on it instead of using `Thread.Sleep`. However, we have used `WaitHandle.WaitAny` to include the cancellation token in the waiting process. So, here we wait for the event or token to be signaled using the 100 ms timeout value and then continue running the loop.

Now the result should be different as follows:

```
WaitHandle task got cancelled in 0 ms
```

Since we are able to proceed with the cancellation as soon as the token gets signaled, it happens almost immediately.

Cancellation using callbacks

It is good when you control all the code, and it is possible to change every piece of the code to implement cancellation properly. However, the most common situation is when you use some external code inside your task and you do not control this code. Imagine if this is connected via a slow network to some server and this fetches data. You press the **Cancel** button, but the operation will not complete until it finishes the I/O operation. This is not a very good user experience and can be a key reason for the user to choose a different software.

Of course, we can write similar code from scratch. However, usually we do not need to, since almost every third-party code such as this provides something, such as the `Close` or `Dispose` methods, allowing us to interrupt communication and release allocated resources. The problem is that these methods can be very different in every third-party framework.

Fortunately, the cancellation API provides us with a possibility to register any cancellation code as a callback and run this callback as soon as a cancellation is requested. To illustrate this approach, we can write a client/server application and implement a callback cancellation.

The server part is relatively simple. We just need to allow inbound connection and simulate a slow response:

```
const int port = 8083;
new Thread(() =>
{
  var listener = new TcpListener(IPAddress.Any, port);
  listener.Start();
  while (true)
    using (var client = listener.AcceptTcpClient())
    using (var stream = client.GetStream())
    using (var writer = new StreamWriter(stream))
```

```
      {
        Thread.Sleep(100);
        writer.WriteLine("OK");
      }
  }) {IsBackground = true}
  .Start();
```

This server will listen for incoming connections on port 8083; when the connection is established, it waits for 100ms and responds with an **OK** string.

Inside our task, we are going to connect to this server via the `TcpClient` class and then cancel the connection as soon as possible:

```
RunTest(tok =>
{
  while (true)
  {
    using (var client = new TcpClient())
    {
      client.Connect("localhost", port);
      using (var stream = client.GetStream())
      using (var reader = new StreamReader(stream))
      Console.WriteLine(reader.ReadLine());
    }
    tok.ThrowIfCancellationRequested();
  }
}, "Callback");
```

This sample prints the following result:

OK

Callback task got cancelled in 109 ms

This code connects to the server and waits for the server to respond; only after getting the response do we proceed with the cancellation.

According to the documentation, the `TcpClient` class includes the `Close` method. This method interrupts work and closes the TCP connection if it has been already opened. All we need to do is to call this method when a cancellation is requested:

```
RunTest(tok =>
{
  while (true)
  {
    using (var client = new TcpClient())
    using (tok.Register(client.Close))
```

```
    {
      client.Connect("localhost", port);
      using (var stream = client.GetStream())
      using (var reader = new StreamReader(stream))
      Console.WriteLine(reader.ReadLine());
    }
    tok.ThrowIfCancellationRequested();
  }
}, "Callback");
```

The difference is just adding a single line of code. We call the `CancellationToken`. `Register` method that accepts the callback that will be called in the case of cancellation and returns the `CancellationTokenRegistration` structure. It implements `IDisposable` and calling the `Dispose` method on it will deregister the callback, so it will not be called if the cancellation happens afterwards.

So in the sample code, we would like to run `client.Close` when the cancellation happens but only inside the inner `using` block. If the cancellation happens somewhere else, we do not need to run this callback. As a result, we will get something like this:

Callback task got cancelled in 3 ms

Now it is clear that we do not wait for the server to respond and cancel the operation almost immediately. We managed to make the users happy without rewriting `TcpClient` from scratch with the help of the cancellation API.

Latency and the coarse-grained approach with TPL

Raw performance, or the number of calculations per second that our program is able to perform, is not always a most important goal to achieve. Sometimes it is even more important to stay responsive and interact with the user as fast as possible. Unfortunately, it is not easy to achieve both these advantages at the same time; there are situations when we need to choose our primary goal.

To simulate such a situation, let's create a combination of coarse-grained computational tasks that takes a long time to complete and runs in the background, and a number of short-lived tasks representing user interaction. We would like these short tasks to run as fast as possible with low latency. Now we write a code to test how these long-running tasks can affect latency:

```
for (var longThreadCount = 0; longThreadCount < 24;
  longThreadCount++)
{
  // Create coarse grained tasks
  var longThreads = new List<Task>();
  for (var i = 0; i < longThreadCount; i++)
    longThreads.Add(
      Task.Factory.StartNew(
        () => Thread.Sleep(1000)));

  // Measure latency
  var sw = Stopwatch.StartNew();
  for (var i = 0; i < _measureCount; i++)
    Task
      .Factory
      .StartNew(() => Thread.SpinWait(100))
      .Wait();
  sw.Stop();
  Console.WriteLine("Long running threads {0}. Average latency
    {1:0.###} ms", longThreadCount,
      (double)sw.ElapsedMilliseconds / _measureCount);

  Task.WaitAll(longThreads.ToArray());
}
```

We have created up to 24 long running threads inside the loop, and in each iteration, we measured up an average latency of running a short task. Finally, we wait for all tasks to complete and print out results. This is how the result data looks on a chart:

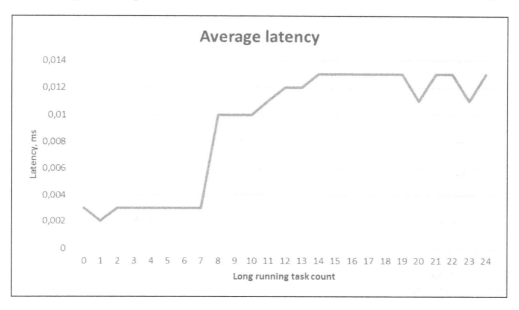

We can see that we have a very low latency until eight long running tasks, and then it dramatically increases up to 4-5 times. The reason is, as usual, complex, but the main reason is that the CPU in this case supports up to eight simultaneously running threads. While long-running tasks occupied fewer threads than this limit, the remaining threads can be used to execute short-lived tasks. As soon as there are no free threads remaining, short tasks have to compete for thread pool worker threads and share CPU time with the long-running tasks, and thus the short tasks become much slower.

To make short tasks faster again, we can isolate long tasks from the thread pool that runs the short tasks. If the short tasks have priority in getting resources, then they will run faster, and the long-running tasks will run a bit slower, but the short-task latency will be much better.

TPL has an option to specify that a task is long-running and should be treated in a special way:

```
Task.Factory.StartNew(
    () => Thread.Sleep(1000),
    TaskCreationOptions.LongRunning)
```

In .NET 4.5, the default task scheduler runs such tasks on separate threads that are not thread pool threads. This is what the reference implementation of the `ThreadPoolTaskScheduler` method of `QueueTask` looks like:

```
protected internal override void QueueTask(Task task)
{
  if ((task.Options & TaskCreationOptions.LongRunning) !=
    TaskCreationOptions.None)
  {
    new Thread(s_longRunningThreadWork) { IsBackground =
      true }.Start(task);
  }
  else
  {
    bool forceGlobal = (task.Options &
      TaskCreationOptions.PreferFairness) !=
        TaskCreationOptions.None;
    ThreadPool.UnsafeQueueCustomWorkItem(task, forceGlobal);
  }
}
```

However, in general, we do not know how such tasks will be treated, and the way of running such tasks is totally up to the current task scheduler implementation.

Adding new results to the chart gives us this:

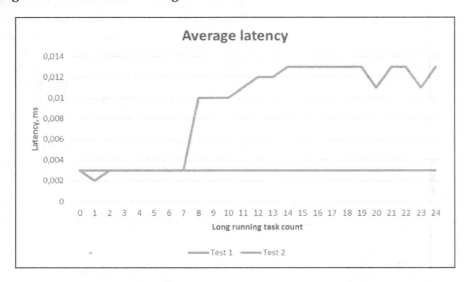

It seems that we successfully resolved latency issue. Of course, the long-running tasks will be slightly slower, but this is what we wanted to achieve.

Exception handling

Another important aspect of TPL is working with exceptions. Just as the normal code that we write can generate an exception, so can the code inside a TPL task. Since every task has its own stack, we cannot work with exceptions in the usual way. TPL has several options that allow us to work with exceptions in a parallel program.

The easiest option is to check the task status. If an exception has been raised inside the task, it will have the `Status` property set to `TaskStatus.Faulted`. The exception will be available through the `Task.Exception` property:

```
var task = Task.Factory.StartNew(() =>
{
  throw new ApplicationException("Test exception");
});

while (!task.IsCompleted) {}

Console.WriteLine("Status = {0}", task.Status);
Console.WriteLine(task.Exception);
```

This code prints the following:

Status = Faulted

System.AggregateException: One or more errors occurred. ---> System.
ApplicationException: Test exception

...

The original exception that has been thrown in the code became wrapped in an `AggregateException` instance. The reason is that there can be many exceptions from child tasks that run in parallel. In the aggregate exception instance, there is the `InnerExceptions` property that will contain all the wrapped exceptions.

To wait for the task completion, we have used a loop instead of the `Task.Wait` method. When a task completes with an exception, this method will rethrow the exception on the thread that has called `Wait`. If we replace the `while` loop with the `task.Wait()` method call and run the code again, we will see an unhandled exception:

Unhandled Exception: System.AggregateException: One or more errors
occurred. ---> System.ApplicationException: Test exception

...

The same behavior will happen when we use the `Task.Result` property or the `Task.WaitAll/WaitAny` static methods.

When reviewing parent-child relations between tasks, we have stated that, if we create a child task with `TaskCreationOptions.AttachedToParent`, then its exceptions will automatically be propagated to the parent task. To check the exception behavior, we can quickly create two nested tasks and throw an exception from the child task:

```
Task.Factory.StartNew(() =>
{
  Task.Factory.StartNew(() =>
  {
    throw new ApplicationException("Test exception");
  }, TaskCreationOptions.AttachedToParent);
})
.Wait();
```

This will print the following:

```
Unhandled Exception: System.AggregateException: One or more errors
occurred. ---> System.AggregateException: One or more errors occurred.
---> System.ApplicationException: Test exception
...
```

As we expected, the parent task completed with the exception that bubbled from its child task. However, now we have an aggregate exception that contains another aggregate exception, which in turn contains the initial exception from the child task. The exception hierarchy repeats the task relationship, which is not always a good thing.

We may put the previous code in a try block and write a catch block to print the inner exceptions as follows:

```
catch (AggregateException ae)
{
  foreach (Exception e in ae.InnerExceptions)
  {
    Console.WriteLine("{0}: {1}", e.GetType(), e.Message);
  }
}
```

The results of the preceding code can be surprising:

```
System.AggregateException: One or more errors occurred.
```

Since it is a hierarchy, we need to check inner exceptions inside each aggregate exception that we get. Since the aggregate exception is only a container for a real exception, we actually need to collect only the other exceptions. Fortunately, there is a way to flatten the exception hierarchy into a simple collection of initial exceptions. To check this, let's create a complex task structure and see what is inside the top-level exception:

```
var t = Task.Factory.StartNew(() =>
{
  Task.Factory.StartNew(
    () =>
    {
      Task.Factory.StartNew(
        () =>
        {
          throw new ApplicationException("And we need to go deeper");
        }, TaskCreationOptions.AttachedToParent);

      throw new ApplicationException("Test exception");
    }, TaskCreationOptions.AttachedToParent);


  Task.Factory.StartNew(() =>
  {
    throw new ApplicationException("Test sibling exception");
  },
  TaskCreationOptions.AttachedToParent);
});
try
{
  t.Wait();
}
catch (AggregateException ae)
{
  foreach (Exception e in ae.Flatten().InnerExceptions)
  {
    Console.WriteLine("{0}: {1}", e.GetType(), e.Message);
  }
}
```

As a result, we will get a list of all the initial exceptions:

```
System.ApplicationException: Test sibling exception
System.ApplicationException: Test exception
System.ApplicationException: And we need to go deeper
```

One of the cancellation options that we have reviewed so far was throwing a special kind of exception, `OperationCanceledException`. TPL treats this exception in a special way. The task status will be `TaskStatus.Canceled` instead of `Faulted`, and the `Exception` property will be empty:

```
var cancelSource = new CancellationTokenSource();
var token = cancelSource.Token;
var task =
  Task
    .Factory
    .StartNew(
      () =>
      {
        while (true)
          token.ThrowIfCancellationRequested();
      },
      token);
while (task.Status != TaskStatus.Running) {}
cancelSource.Cancel();
while (!task.IsCompleted) {}
Console.WriteLine("Status = {0}, IsCanceled = {1}", task.Status, task.
IsCanceled);
Console.WriteLine(task.Exception);
```

The result shows that a cancellation exception in this case is being treated differently:

```
Status = Canceled, IsCanceled = True
```

 Please notice that if we do not pass a token instance as the last parameter of the StartNew method, the cancellation exception will be treated like a regular exception.

Using the Parallel class

TPL provides a reach API to compose a parallel program. However, it is quite verbose, and if we write a simple code, there are easier way to parallelize it. For common tasks such as running some code in parallel and parallelizing the `for` and `foreach` loops, there is a Parallel class that provides a simple and easy to use API.

Parallel.Invoke

This method executes actions in parallel if the CPU has multiple cores and supports multiple threads. If the CPU has only one core, actions will be executed synchronously. This method blocks the calling thread until all the actions are completed:

```
Parallel.Invoke(
  () => Console.WriteLine("Action 1"),
  () =>
  {
    Thread.SpinWait(10000);
    Console.WriteLine("Action 2");
  },
  () => Console.WriteLine("Action 3"));
Console.WriteLine("End");
```

After running the preceding lines of code, we get the following output:

Action 1

Action 3

Action 2

End

We can provide the `ParallelOptions` class instance to this method to configure additional options such as limiting the parallelism degree, specifying a cancellation token, and using a specific implementation of the task scheduler to run tasks on it.

The straightforward implementation of this method will be as follows:

```
var tasks = new List<Task>();

foreach (var action in actions)
{
  tasks.Add(Task.Factory.StartNew(action));
}

Task.WaitAll(tasks.ToArray());
```

However, the real implementation, besides cancellation, correctness checks, and exception handling, is still very different. This is due to code performance optimization. The usual task scheduler is written assuming that we do not know how many tasks we are going to run. In this specific case, this is a defined value. If it is less than or equal to SMALL_ACTIONCOUNT_LIMIT (that is 10 in the current .NET Framework version 4.5), then the algorithm is similar to our implementation.

In the case of more tasks, it becomes more complicated. First, we create an empty special task called **replicable task**. This task is treated in a special way by a task scheduler. The implementation code is as follows:

```
var actionIndex = 0;
var rootTask =
  new ReplicableTask(
    () =>
    {
      int myIndex;
      while ((myIndex = InterLocked.Increment(ref actionIndex)) <=
        actions.Length)
        body(myIndex-1);
    });
rootTask.RunSynchronously();
rootTask.Wait();
```

Here, we have the `actionIndex` local variable that is used by the task code inside the lambda expression. This creates a closure, and the C# compiler generates a helper class instance and puts the `actionIndex` variable inside this class as a field. Thus, if we create more copies of this task, they all will share a single `actionIndex` variable. At the same time, the `myIndex` variable will be different for each copy of this task.

So a scheduling algorithm can create as many copies of this task as needed, and still it is guaranteed that every action will be executed at least once or only one time. This allows scheduling mechanisms to work efficiently. First, we create as many copies of the threads as the CPU support. Then, if tasks run longer than a certain amount of time, the scheduler will create more copies to prevent CPU cores from idling. This makes the tasks run slightly slower, but we know that our tasks are long-running and this will not be important for overall performance.

This algorithm also ensures that, even when we have many actions to be run, the real number of tasks that are to be executed in parallel will be low and close to the number of threads that the CPU supports.

Parallel.For and Parallel.Foreach

These methods are useful to create parallel loops. They use the same strategy as `Parallel.Invoke`, since it is very effective when having a large number of iterations to run in parallel. `Parallel.Foreach` offers even more control, allowing us to use a custom task partitioning algorithm with the `Partitioner<T>` and `OrderablePartitioner<T>` abstract class implementations.

To see the default parallelization strategy, let's run this code:

```
private static void Calc(int iterations)
{
  var taskIds = new HashSet<int>();
  var sum = 0;
  Parallel.For(
    0,
    iterations,
    i =>
    {
      Thread.SpinWait(1000000);
      lock (taskIds)
        taskIds.Add(Task.CurrentId.Value);
    });
  Console.WriteLine("{0} iterations, {1} tasks", iterations,
    taskIds.Count);
}
```

We simply call the `Parallel.For` method with a different number of iterations and count how many unique task ids we've got.

On a machine with Core i7-2600K CPU, we will get these values:

```
1 iteration, 1 tasks
4 iterations, 4 tasks
8 iterations, 8 tasks
12 iterations, 8 tasks
16 iterations, 8 tasks
32 iterations, 9 tasks
64 iterations, 9 tasks
```

The CPU supports eight concurrent threads, and the algorithm chose eight tasks to run in parallel until 32 iterations, when one additional task is added to prevent possible CPU idling; this makes the code more efficient.

Understanding the task scheduler

The task scheduler manages and executes TPL tasks. First, we will review a default task scheduler algorithm, and then we will learn how to create a custom task scheduler and use it with TPL to run tasks on it.

The default task scheduler is based on the .NET thread pool and uses its global queue to run top-level tasks that are not created in the context of another task. However, if we create a nested or child task, it is put on a local queue that is created on a worker thread that runs the parent task. When this worker thread gets ready to run a task, it first looks for work items on the local queue that is accessed in LIFO order. Using local queue reduces contention since we do not access any shared data; thus, there is no need for any synchronization.

If the local queue is empty, the worker thread looks into a global queue. If this queue is empty, then to prevent idling the thread is going to look at other threads' local queues. If the thread finds a work item here after running some heuristics to decide if taking this work item will be efficient, the thread steals this work item from another thread's local queue. The stealing happens in FIFO order for efficiency reasons.

This way TPL tries to improve performance by lowering contention and using CPU cache more effectively, and at the same time, by load balancing between worker threads with a work-stealing algorithm.

The default scheduler works well, but in some cases, we need to replace it with another. Imagine a WPF application that has a button clicked event handler with the following code:

```
var t = Task.Factory.StartNew(() =>
{
  Console.WriteLine("Id: {0}, Is threadpool thread: {1}",
    Thread.CurrentThread.ManagedThreadId,
    Thread.CurrentThread.IsThreadPoolThread);

  Thread.Sleep(TimeSpan.FromSeconds(1));
  _label.Content = new TextBlock {Text = "Hello from TPL task"};
},
CancellationToken.None,
TaskCreationOptions.None,
TaskScheduler.Default);

while (t.Status != TaskStatus.RanToCompletion && t.Status !=
TaskStatus.Faulted)
{
  // run message loop
  Application.Current.Dispatcher.Invoke(
    DispatcherPriority.Background, new Action(delegate { }));
}

if (null != t.Exception)
{
```

```
    var innerException = t.Exception.Flatten().InnerException;
    Console.WriteLine("{0}: {1}", innerException.GetType(),
      innerException.Message);
}
```

If we run this code, we will see the following:

Id: 4, Is threadpool thread: True

System.InvalidOperationException: The calling thread must be STA, because many UI components require this.

The reason is that we tried to access the UI control from a thread pool worker thread, which is forbidden. To make this code work, we have to use a task scheduler that will put this task on a UI thread:

```
var t = Task.Factory.StartNew(() =>
{
    Console.WriteLine("Id: {0}, Is threadpool thread: {1}",
      Thread.CurrentThread.ManagedThreadId,
      Thread.CurrentThread.IsThreadPoolThread);

    Thread.Sleep(TimeSpan.FromSeconds(1));
    _label.Content = new TextBlock {Text = "Hello from TPL task"};
    },
    CancellationToken.None,
    TaskCreationOptions.None,
  TaskScheduler.FromCurrentSynchronizationContext());
```

The output will be different, and the program will run successfully, changing the label value:

Id: 1, Is threadpool thread: False

The UI and asynchrony is a very large and complicated topic. We will get back to this later in this book.

Last but not the least is implementing a custom task scheduler. We need to inherit this from the TaskScheduler class and implement several abstract members:

```
public class SynchronousTaskScheduler: TaskScheduler
{
  // we do not schedule tasks, we run them synchronously
  protected override IEnumerable<Task> GetScheduledTasks()
  {
    return Enumerable.Empty<Task>();
  }
```

```
// run the task synchronously on the current thread
protected override void QueueTask(Task task)
{
  TryExecuteTask(task);
}

// the same thing - just run the task on current thread
protected override bool TryExecuteTaskInline(
  Task task, bool taskWasPreviouslyQueued)
{
  return TryExecuteTask(task);
}

// maximum concurrency level is 1, because only one task runs at
//a time
public override int MaximumConcurrencyLevel
{
  get { return 1; }
}
}
```

Of course, real-world task schedulers are much more complicated than this one, but this works too. Let's use this with the previous code:

```
var t = Task.Factory.StartNew(() =>
{
  Console.WriteLine("Id: {0}, Is threadpool thread: {1}",
    Thread.CurrentThread.ManagedThreadId,
    Thread.CurrentThread.IsThreadPoolThread);

  Thread.Sleep(TimeSpan.FromSeconds(1));
  _label.Content = new TextBlock {Text = "Hello from TPL task"};
  },
  CancellationToken.None,
  TaskCreationOptions.None,
  new SynchronousTaskScheduler());
```

The code will work fine and we will get the same results.

Summary

In this chapter, we have reviewed Task Parallel Library in detail. We have studied its architecture and composition blocks. We have learned about exception handling and task cancellation in detail. We examined performance and latency issues by finding out the best way of writing code to achieve good results. Using the `Parallel` class API allowed us to quickly create parallel programs, and deep-diving into TPL task scheduling allowed us to write a custom task scheduler and customize TPL task execution.

In the next chapter, we will learn how the C# language supports asynchrony. We will understand its new keywords, `async` and `await`, and understand how we can use Task Parallel Library with the new C# syntax. Also, we will review in detail how exactly new language features work and create our own custom code that will be compatible with the `await` statement.

5

C# Language Support for Asynchrony

The **Task Parallel Library** makes it possible to combine asynchronous tasks and set dependencies between them. In the previous chapter, we reviewed this topic in detail. However to get a clear understanding in this chapter, we will use this approach to solve a real problem—downloading images from Bing (the search engine). Also, we will do the following:

- Implement standard synchronous approach
- Use Task Parallel Library to create an asynchronous version of the program
- Use C# 5.0 built-in asynchrony support to make the code easier to read and maintain
- Simulate C# asynchronous infrastructure with the help of iterators
- Learn about other useful features of Task Parallel Library
- Make any C# type compatible with built-in asynchronous keywords

Implementing the downloading of images from Bing

Everyday `Bing.com` publishes its background image that can be used as desktop wallpaper. There is an XML API to get information about these pictures that can be found at `http://www.bing.com/hpimagearchive.aspx`.

Creating a simple synchronous solution

Let's try to write a program to download the last eight images from this site. We will
start by defining objects to store image information. This is where a thumbnail image
and its description will be stored:

```
using System.Drawing;

public class WallpaperInfo
{
  private readonly Image _thumbnail;
  private readonly string _description;

  public WallpaperInfo(Image thumbnail, string description)
  {
    _thumbnail = thumbnail;
    _description = description;
  }

  public Image Thumbnail
  {
    get { return _thumbnail; }
  }

  public string Description
  {
    get { return _description; }
  }
}
```

The next container type is for all the downloaded pictures and the time required to
download and make the thumbnail images from the original pictures:

```
public class WallpapersInfo
{
  private readonly long _milliseconds;
  private readonly WallpaperInfo[] _wallpapers;

  public WallpapersInfo(long milliseconds, WallpaperInfo[]
    wallpapers)
  {
    _milliseconds = milliseconds;
    _wallpapers = wallpapers;
  }
}
```

```
public long Milliseconds
{
  get { return _milliseconds; }
}

public WallpaperInfo[] Wallpapers
{
  get { return _wallpapers; }
}
}
```

Now we need to create a loader class to download images from Bing. We need to define a `Loader` static class and follow with an implementation. Let's create a method that will make a thumbnail image from the source image stream:

```
private static Image GetThumbnail(Stream imageStream)
{
  using (imageStream)
  {
    var fullBitmap = Image.FromStream(imageStream);
    return new Bitmap(fullBitmap, 192, 108);
  }
}
```

To communicate via the HTTP protocol, it is recommended to use the `System.Net.HttpClient` type from the `System.Net.dll` assembly. Let's create the following extension methods that will allow us to use the POST HTTP method to download an image and get an opened stream:

```
private static Stream DownloadData(this HttpClient client, string uri)
{
  var response = client.PostAsync(
    uri, new StringContent(string.Empty)).Result;

  return response.Content.ReadAsStreamAsync().Result;
}

private static Task<Stream> DownloadDataAsync(this HttpClient
  client, string uri){
  Task<HttpResponseMessage> responseTask = client.PostAsync(
    uri, new StringContent(string.Empty));

  return responseTask.ContinueWith(task =>
    task.Result.Content.ReadAsStreamAsync()).Unwrap();
}
```

To create the easiest implementation possible, we will implement downloading without any asynchrony. Here, we will define HTTP endpoints for the Bing API:

```
private const string _catalogUri =
  "http://www.bing.com/hpimagearchive.aspx?
    format=xml&idx=0&n=8&mbl=1&mkt=en-ww";
private const string _imageUri =
  "http://bing.com{0}_1920x1080.jpg";
```

Then, we will start measuring the time required to finish downloading and download an XML catalog that has information about the images that we need:

```
var sw = Stopwatch.StartNew();

var client = new HttpClient();
var catalogXmlString = client.DownloadString(_catalogUri);
```

Next, the XML string will be parsed to an XML document:

```
var xDoc = XDocument.Parse(catalogXmlString);
```

Now using LINQ to XML, we will query the information needed from the document and run the download process for each image:

```
var wallpapers = xDoc
  .Root
  .Elements("image")
  .Select(e =>
    new
    {
      Desc = e.Element("copyright").Value,
      Url = e.Element("urlBase").Value
    })
  .Select(item =>
    new
    {
      item.Desc,
      FullImageData = client.DownloadData(
        string.Format(_imageUri, item.Url))
    })
  .Select( item =>
    new WallpaperInfo(
      GetThumbnail(item.FullImageData),
      item.Desc))
  .ToArray();

sw.Stop();
```

The first `Select` method call extracts the image URL and description from each `image` XML element that is a direct child of root element. This information is contained inside the `urlBase` and `copyright` XML elements inside the `image` element. The second one downloads an image from the Bing site. The last `Select` method creates a thumbnail image and stores all the information needed inside the `WallPaperInfo` class instance.

To display the results, we need to create a user interface. **Windows Forms** is a simple and fast way to implement the technology, so we can use it to show the results to the user. There is a button that runs the download, a panel to show the downloaded pictures, and a label that will show the time required to finish downloading.

Here is the implementation code. This includes a calculation of the top co-ordinate for each element, a code to display the images and start the download process:

```
private int GetItemTop(int height, int index)
{
  return index * (height + 8) + 8;
}

private void RefreshContent(WallpapersInfo info)
{
  _resultPanel.Controls.Clear();
  _resultPanel.Controls.AddRange(
  info.Wallpapers.SelectMany((wallpaper, i) => new Control[]
  {
    new PictureBox
    {
      Left = 4,
      Image = wallpaper.Thumbnail,
      AutoSize = true,
      Top = GetItemTop(wallpaper.Thumbnail.Height, i)
    },
    new Label
    {
      Left = wallpaper.Thumbnail.Width + 8,
      Top = GetItemTop(wallpaper.Thumbnail.Height, i),
      Text = wallpaper.Description,
      AutoSize = true
    }
  }).ToArray());

  _timeLabel.Text = string.Format(
    "Time: {0}ms", info.Milliseconds);
```

```
    }
    private void _loadSyncBtn_Click(object sender, System.EventArgs e)
    {
      var info = Loader.SyncLoad();
      RefreshContent(info);
    }
```

The result looks as follows:

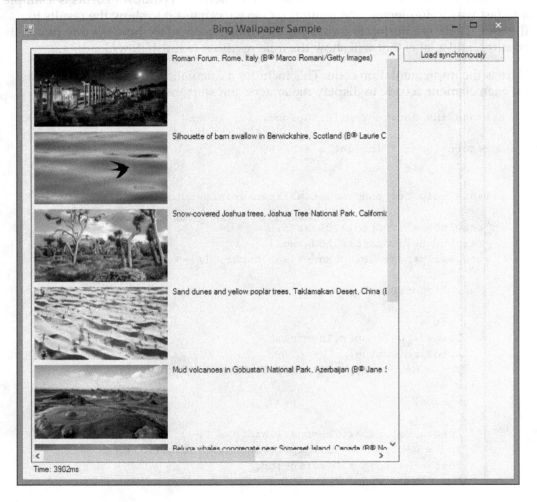

So the time to download all these images should be about several seconds if the Internet connection is broadband. Can we do this faster? We certainly can! Now we will download and process the images one by one, but we totally can process each image in parallel.

Creating a parallel solution with Task Parallel Library

In the previous chapter, we reviewed Task Parallel Library and the relationships between tasks. The code naturally splits into several stages:

- Load images catalog XML from Bing
- Parse the XML document and get the information needed about the images
- Load each image's data from Bing
- Create a thumbnail image for each image downloaded

The process can be visualized with the dependency chart:

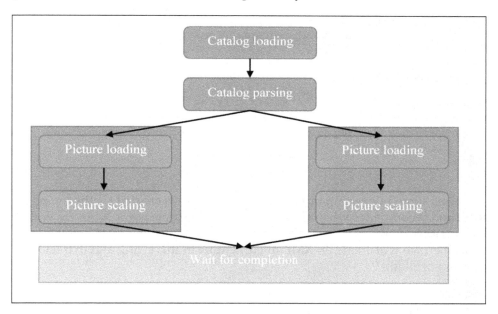

`HttpClient` has naturally asynchronous API, so we only need to combine everything together with the help of a `Task.ContinueWith` method:

```
public static Task<WallpapersInfo> TaskLoad()
{
    var sw = Stopwatch.StartNew();

    var downloadBingXmlTask = new HttpClient().GetStringAsync(
        _catalogUri);

    var parseXmlTask = downloadBingXmlTask.ContinueWith(task =>
```

```csharp
    {
        var xmlDocument = XDocument.Parse(task.Result);
        return xmlDocument.Root
            .Elements("image")
            .Select(e =>
                new
                {
                    Description = e.Element("copyright").Value,
                    Url = e.Element("urlBase").Value
                });
    });

    var downloadImagesTask = parseXmlTask.ContinueWith(
        task => Task.WhenAll(
            task.Result.Select(item => new HttpClient()
                .DownloadDataAsync(string.Format(_imageUri, item.Url))
                .ContinueWith(downloadTask => new WallpaperInfo(
                    GetThumbnail(downloadTask.Result), item.Description)))))
                .Unwrap();

    return downloadImagesTask.ContinueWith(task =>
    {
        sw.Stop();

        return new WallpapersInfo(sw.ElapsedMilliseconds,
            task.Result);
    });
}
```

The code has some interesting moments. The first task is created by the `HttpClient` instance, and it completes when the download process succeeds. Now we will attach a subsequent task, which will use the XML string downloaded by the previous task, and then we will create an XML document from this string and extract the information needed.

Now this is becoming more complicated. We want to create a task to download each image and continue until all these tasks complete successfully. So we will use the LINQ Select method to run downloads for each image that was defined in the XML catalog, and after the download process completes, we will create a thumbnail image and store the information in the `WallpaperInfo` instance. This creates `IEnumerable<Task<WallpaperInfo>>` as a result, and to wait for all these tasks to complete, we will use the `Task.WhenAll` method. However, this is a task that is inside a continuation task, and the result is going to be of the `Task<Task<WallpaperInfo[]>>` type. To get the inner task, we will use the `Unwrap` method, which has the following syntax:

```csharp
public static Task Unwrap(this Task<Task> task)
```

This can be used on any `Task<Task>` instance and will create a proxy task that represents an entire asynchronous operation properly.

The last task is to stop the timer and return the downloaded images and is quite straightforward. We have to add another button to the UI to run this implementation. Notice the implementation of the button click handler:

```
private void _loadTaskBtn_Click(object sender, System.EventArgs e)
{
  var info = Loader.TaskLoad();
  info.ContinueWith(task => RefreshContent(task.Result),
    CancellationToken.None,
    TaskContinuationOptions.None,
    TaskScheduler.FromCurrentSynchronizationContext());
}
```

Since the `TaskLoad` method is asynchronous, it returns immediately. To display the results, we have to define a continuation task. However, from the previous chapter you already know that the default task scheduler will run a task code on a thread pool worker thread. To work with UI controls, we have to run the code on the UI thread, and we use a task scheduler that captures the current synchronization context and runs the continuation task on this. We will cover synchronization context and the related infrastructure later in *Chapter 8, Server-Side Asynchrony*, and *Chapter 9, Concurrency in the User Interface*, where server-side and client-side asynchrony will be reviewed in detail.

Let's name the button as **Load using TPL** and test the results. If your Internet connection is fast, this implementation will download the images in parallel much faster compared to the previous sequential download process.

If we look back at the code, we will see that it is quite hard to understand what it actually does. We can see how one task depends on the other, but the original goal is unclear despite the code being very compact and easy. Imagine what will happen if we try to add exception handling here. We would have to append an additional continuation task with exception handling to each task. This will be much harder to read and understand. In a real-world program, it will be a challenging task to keep in mind these tasks composition and support a code written in such a paradigm.

Enhancing the code with C# 5.0 built-in support for asynchrony

Fortunately, C# 5.0 introduced the `async` and `await` keywords that are intended to make asynchronous code look synchronous, and thus, makes reading of code and understanding the program flow easier. However, this is another abstraction and it hides many things that happen under the hood from the programmer, which in several situations is not a good thing. The potential pitfalls and solutions will be covered later in this book, but now let's rewrite the previous code using new C# 5.0 features:

```csharp
public static async Task<WallpapersInfo> AsyncLoad()
{
  var sw = Stopwatch.StartNew();

  var client = new HttpClient();
  var catalogXmlString = await client.GetStringAsync(_catalogUri);
  var xDoc = XDocument.Parse(catalogXmlString);

  var wallpapersTask = xDoc
    .Root
    .Elements("image")
    .Select(e =>
      new
      {
        Description = e.Element("copyright").Value,
        Url = e.Element("urlBase").Value
      })
    .Select(async item =>
      new
      {
        item.Description,
        FullImageData = await client.DownloadDataAsync(
          string.Format(_imageUri, item.Url))
      });

  var wallpapersItems = await Task.WhenAll(wallpapersTask);

  var wallpapers = wallpapersItems.Select(
    item => new WallpaperInfo(
      GetThumbnail(item.FullImageData), item.Description));

  sw.Stop();

  return new WallpapersInfo(sw.ElapsedMilliseconds,
    wallpapers.ToArray());
}
```

Now the code looks almost like the first synchronous implementation. The AsyncLoad method has a async modifier and a Task<T> return value, and such methods must always return Task or be declared as void—this is enforced by the compiler. However, in the method's code, the type that is returned is just T. This is strange at first, but the method's return value will be eventually turned into Task<T> by the C# 5.0 compiler. The async modifier is necessary to use await inside the method. In the further code, there is await inside a lambda expression, and we need to mark this lambda as async as well.

So what is going on when we use await inside our code? It does not always mean that the call is actually asynchronous. It can happen that by the time we call the method, the result is already available, so we just get the result and proceed further. However, the most common case is when we make an asynchronous call. In this case, we start, for example, by downloading a XML string from Bing via HTTP and immediately return a task that is a continuation task and contains the rest of the code after the line with await.

To run this, we need to add another button named **Load using async**. We are going to use await in the button click event handler as well, so we need to mark it with the async modifier:

```
private async void _loadAsyncBtn_Click(object sender,
    System.EventArgs e)
{
    var info = await Loader.AsyncLoad();
    RefreshContent(info);
}
```

Now if the code after await is being run in a continuation task, why is there no multithreaded access exception? The RefreshContent method runs in another task, but the C# compiler is aware of the synchronization context and generates a code that executes the continuation task on the UI thread. The result should be as fast as a TPL implementation but the code is much cleaner and easy to follow.

Last but not least, is the possibility to put asynchronous method calls inside a try block. The C# compiler generates a code that will propagate the exception into the current context and unwrap the AggregateException instance to get the original exception from it.

 In C# 5.0, it was impossible to use await inside catch and finally blocks, but C# 6.0 introduced a new async/await infrastructure and this limitation was removed.

Simulating C# asynchronous infrastructure with iterators

To dig into the implementation details, it makes sense to look at the decompiled code of the `AsyncLoad` method:

```
public static Task<WallpapersInfo> AsyncLoad()
{
  Loader.<AsyncLoad>d__21 stateMachine;

  stateMachine.<>t__builder =
    AsyncTaskMethodBuilder<WallpapersInfo>.Create();

  stateMachine.<>1__state = -1;

  stateMachine
    .<>t__builder
    .Start<Loader.<AsyncLoad>d__21>(ref stateMachine);

  return stateMachine.<>t__builder.Task;
}
```

The method body was replaced by a compiler-generated code that creates a special kind of state machine. We will not review the further implementation details here, because it is quite complicated and is subject to changes from version to version. However, what's going on is that the code gets divided into separate pieces at each line where `await` is present, and each piece becomes a separate state in the generated state machine. Then, a special `System.Runtime.CompilerServices.AsyncTaskMethodBuilder` structure creates `Task` that represents the generated state machine workflow.

This state machine is quite similar to the one that is generated for the iterator methods that leverage the `yield` keyword. In C# 6.0, the same universal code gets generated for the code containing `yield` and `await`. To illustrate the general principles behind the generated code, we can use iterator methods to implement another version of asynchronous images download from Bing.

Therefore, we can turn an asynchronous method into an iterator method that returns the `IEnumerable<Task>` instance. We replace each `await` with `yield return` making each iteration to be returned as `Task`. To run such a method, we need to execute each task and return the final result. This code can be considered as an analogue of `AsyncTaskMethodBuilder`:

```
private static Task<TResult> ExecuteIterator<TResult>(
  Func<Action<TResult>,IEnumerable<Task>> iteratorGetter)
{
  return Task.Run(() =>
  {
    var result = default(TResult);

    foreach (var task in iteratorGetter(res => result = res))
      task.Wait();

    return result;
  });
}
```

We iterate through each task and await its completion. Since we cannot use the `out` and `ref` parameters in iterator methods, we use a lambda expression to return the result from each task. To make the code easier to understand, we have created a new container task and used the `foreach` loop; however, to be closer to the original implementation, we should get the first task and use the `ContinueWith` method providing the next task to it and continue until the last task. In this case, we will end up having one final task representing an entire sequence of asynchronous operations, but the code will become more complicated as well.

Since it is not possible to use the yield keyword inside a lambda expressions in the current C# versions, we will implement image download and thumbnail generation as a separate method:

```
private static IEnumerable<Task> GetImageIterator(
  string url,
  string desc,
  Action<WallpaperInfo> resultSetter)
{
  var loadTask = new HttpClient().DownloadDataAsync(
    string.Format(_imageUri, url));

  yield return loadTask;

  var thumbTask = Task.FromResult(GetThumbnail(loadTask.Result));
  yield return thumbTask;

  resultSetter(new WallpaperInfo(thumbTask.Result, desc));
}
```

It looks like a common C# async code with `yield return` used instead of the `await` keyword and `resultSetter` used instead of `return`. Notice the `Task.FromResult` method that we used to get `Task` from the synchronous `GetThumbnail` method. We can use `Task.Run` and put this operation on a separate worker thread, but it will be an ineffective solution. `Task.FromResult` allows us to get `Task` that is already completed and has a result. If you use `await` with such task, it will be translated into a synchronous call.

The main code can be rewritten in the same way:

```
private static IEnumerable<Task> GetWallpapersIterator(
  Action<WallpaperInfo[]> resultSetter)
{
  var catalogTask = new HttpClient().GetStringAsync(_catalogUri);
  yield return catalogTask;

  var xDoc = XDocument.Parse(catalogTask.Result);

  var imagesTask = Task.WhenAll(xDoc
    .Root
    .Elements("image")
    .Select(e => new
    {
      Description = e.Element("copyright").Value,
      Url = e.Element("urlBase").Value
    })
    .Select(item => ExecuteIterator<WallpaperInfo>(
      resSetter => GetImageIterator(
        item.Url, item.Description, resSetter))));

  yield return imagesTask;

  resultSetter(imagesTask.Result);
}
```

This combines everything together:

```
public static WallpapersInfo IteratorLoad()
{
  var sw = Stopwatch.StartNew();

  var wallpapers = ExecuteIterator<WallpaperInfo[]>(
    GetWallpapersIterator)
      .Result;

  sw.Stop();

  return new WallpapersInfo(sw.ElapsedMilliseconds, wallpapers);
}
```

To run this, we will create one more button called **Load using iterator**. The button click handler just runs the `IteratorLoad` method and then refreshes the UI. This also works with about the same speed as other asynchronous implementations.

This example can help us to understand the logic behind the C# code generation for asynchronous methods used with `await`. Of course, the real code is much more complicated, but the principles behind it remain the same.

Is the async keyword really needed?

It is a common question about why do we need to mark methods as `async`. We have already mentioned iterator methods in C# and the `yield` keyword. This is very similar to `async/await`, and yet we do not need to mark iterator methods with any modifier. The C# compiler is able to determine that it is an iterator method when it meets the `yield return` or `yield break` operators inside such a method. So the question is, why is it not the same with `await` and the asynchronous methods?

The reason is that asynchrony support was introduced in the latest C# version, and it is very important not to break any legacy code while changing the language. Imagine if any code used `await` as a name for a field or variable. If C# developers make `await` a keyword without any conditions, this old code will break and stop compiling. The current approach guarantees that if we do not mark a method with `async`, the old code will continue to work.

Fire-and-forget tasks

Besides `Task` and `Task<T>`, we can declare an asynchronous method as void. It is useful in the case of top-level event handlers, for example, the button click or text changed handlers in the UI. An event handler that returns a value is possible, but is very inconvenient to use and does not make much sense.

So allowing `async void` methods makes it possible to use `await` inside such event handlers:

```
private async void button1_Click(object sender, EventArgs e)
{
    await SomeAsyncStuff();
}
```

It seems that nothing bad is happening, and the C# compiler generates almost the same code as for the `Task` returning method, but there is an important catch related to exceptions handling.

When an asynchronous method returns `Task`, exceptions are connected to this task and can be handled both by TPL and the `try`/`catch` block in case `await` is used. However, if we have a `async void` method, we have no `Task` to attach the exceptions to and those exceptions just get posted to the current synchronization context. These exceptions can be observed using `AppDomain.UnhandledException` or similar events in a GUI application, but this is very easy to miss and not a good practice.

The other problem is that we cannot use a `void` returning asynchronous method with `await`, since there is no return value that can be used to await on it. We cannot compose such a method with other asynchronous tasks and participate in the program workflow. It is basically a fire-and-forget operation that we start, and then we have no way to control how it will proceed (if we did not write the code for this explicitly).

Another problem is `void` returning `async` lambda expression. It is very hard to notice that lambda returns void, and all problems related to usual methods are related to lambda expression as well. Imagine that we want to run some operation in parallel. From the previous chapter we learned that to achieve this, we can use the `Parallel.ForEach` method. To download some news in parallel, we can write a code like this:

```
Parallel.ForEach(Enumerable.Range(1,10), async i =>
{
  var news = await newsClient.GetTopNews(i);
  newsCollection.Add(news);
});
```

However, this will not work, because the second parameter of the `ForEach` method is `Action<T>`, which is a void returning delegate. Thus, we will spawn 10 download processes, but since we cannot wait for completion, we abandon all asynchronous operations that we just started and ignore the results.

A general rule of thumb is to avoid using `async void` methods. If this is inevitable and there is an event handler, then always wrap the inner `await` method calls in try/catch blocks and provide exception handling.

Other useful TPL features

Task Parallel Library has a large codebase and some useful features such as `Task.Unwrap` or `Task.FromResult` that are not very well known to developers. We have still not mentioned two more extremely useful methods yet. They are covered in the following sections.

Task.Delay

Often, it is required to wait for a certain amount of time in the code. One of the traditional ways to wait is using the `Thread.Sleep` method. The problem is that `Thread.Sleep` blocks the current thread, and it is not asynchronous.

Another disadvantage is that we cannot cancel waiting if something has happened. To implement a solution for this, we will have to use system synchronization primitives such as an event, but this is not very easy to code. To keep the code simple, we can use the `Task.Delay` method:

```
// Do something
await Task.Delay(1000);
// Do something
```

This method can be canceled with a help of the `CancellationToken` infrastructure and uses system timer under the hood, so this kind of waiting is truly asynchronous.

Task.Yield

Sometimes we need a part of the code to be guaranteed to run asynchronously. For example, we need to keep the UI responsive, or maybe we would like to implement a fine-grained scenario. Anyway, as we already know that using `await` does not mean that the call will be asynchronous. If we want to return control immediately and run the rest of the code as a continuation task, we can use the `Task.Yield` method:

```
// Do something
await Task.Yield();
// Do something
```

`Task.Yield` just causes a continuation to be posted on the current synchronization context, or if the synchronization context is not available, a continuation will be posted on a thread pool worker thread.

Implementing a custom awaitable type

Until now we have only used `Task` with the `await` operator. However, it is not the only type that is compatible with `await`. Actually, the `await` operator can be used with every type that contains the `GetAwaiter` method with no parameters and the return type that does the following:

- Implements the `INotifyCompletion` interface
- Contains the `IsCompleted` boolean property
- Has the `GetResult` method with no parameters

This method can even be an extension method, so it is possible to extend the existing types and add the await compatibility to them. In this example, we will create such a method for the Uri type. This method will download content as a string via HTTP from the address provided in the Uri instance:

```
private static TaskAwaiter<string> GetAwaiter(this Uri url)
{
    return new HttpClient().GetStringAsync(url).GetAwaiter();
}

var content = await new Uri("http://google.com");
Console.WriteLine(content.Substring(0, 10));
```

If we run this, we will see the first 10 characters of the Google website content.

As you may notice, here we used the Task type indirectly, returning the already provided awaiter method for the Task type. We can implement an awaiter method manually from scratch, but it really does not make any sense. To understand how this works it will be enough to create a custom wrapper around an already existing TaskAwaiter:

```
struct DownloadAwaiter : INotifyCompletion
{
    private readonly TaskAwaiter<string> _awaiter;

    public DownloadAwaiter(Uri uri)
    {
        Console.WriteLine("Start downloading from {0}", uri);
        var task = new HttpClient().GetStringAsync(uri);
        _awaiter = task.GetAwaiter();
        Task.GetAwaiter().OnCompleted(() => Console.WriteLine(
            "download completed"));
    }

    public bool IsCompleted
    {
        get { return _awaiter.IsCompleted; }
    }

    public void OnCompleted(Action continuation)
    {
        _awaiter.OnCompleted(continuation);
    }

    public string GetResult()
    {
        return _awaiter.GetResult();
    }
}
```

With this code, we have customized asynchronous execution that provides diagnostic information to the console. To get rid of `TaskAwaiter`, it will be enough to change the `OnCompleted` method with custom code that will execute some operation and then a continuation provided in this method.

To use this custom awaiter, we need to change `GetAwaiter` accordingly:

```
private static DownloadAwaiter GetAwaiter(this Uri uri)
{
    return new DownloadAwaiter(uri);
}
```

If we run this, we will see additional information on the console. This can be useful for diagnostics and debugging.

Summary

In this chapter, we looked at the C# language infrastructure that supports asynchronous calls. We covered the new C# keywords, `async` and `await`, and how we can use Task Parallel Library with the new C# syntax. We learned how C# generates code and creates a state machine that represents an asynchronous operation, and we implemented an analogue solution with the help of iterator methods and the `yield` keyword. Besides this, we studied additional Task Parallel Library features and looked at how we can use `await` with any custom type.

In the next chapter, we will learn about data structures that are built for concurrency and common algorithms that rely on them.

6
Using Concurrent Data Structures

Choosing an appropriate data structure for your concurrent algorithm is a crucial step. We have already learned from the previous chapters that it is not usually possible to use just any .NET object as a shared data in a multithreaded program. We can assume that most of the common types in .NET are implemented in such a way that their static members are thread-safe, while their instance members are not. However, only those objects that are specifically designed to be thread-safe can be used as they are in a multithreaded environment.

Therefore, if we need multiple threads to add some item to a collection, we cannot just call the `Add` method of a shared instance of the `List<T>` type. It will lead to unpredictable results, and most probably the program will end up throwing a weird exception.

Thus, in this situation, there are two general ways to follow: either we implement synchronized access to the standard collection ourselves with the help of existing synchronization primitives, or we can use existing concurrent collections from the `System.Collections.Concurrent` namespace.

In this chapter, we are going to dig into the details of using data structures in concurrent applications and review advantages and disadvantages of each option.

Standard collections and synchronization primitives

To highlight what problems can appear when we use nonthread safe collections in a concurrent program, let's write a simple program that will use the `Parallel.Foreach` class to copy a collection and double its elements:

```
var source = Enumerable.Range(1, 42000).ToList();
var destination = new List<int>();

Parallel.ForEach(source, n => destination.Add(n * 2));

Assert.AreEqual(source.Count, destination.Count);
```

If we run this code, we will almost certainly get the `AggregateException` exception with the `ArgumentException` instance wrapped inside it.

This happens because the `Add` method of the `List<T>` class is not thread safe, and the reason for this lies in the implementation details:

```
public void Add(T item)
{
    if (_size == _items.Length) EnsureCapacity(_size + 1);
    _items[_size++] = item;
    _version++;
}
```

In case the concurrent threads access this method when the `_size == items.Length - 1` condition is true, the `ArgumentException` exception will almost certainly occur. The implementation will cause the collection to have an inconsistent state; a race condition will lead the inner array new size to be less than needed.

To avoid a race condition, we can implement some sort of synchronization for shared collection access using the **lock** statement:

```
object syncRoot = new object();
var source = Enumerable.Range(1, 42000).ToList();
var destination = new List<int>();

Parallel.ForEach(source,
    n =>
    {
        lock (syncRoot)
        {
            destination.Add(n * 2);
```

```
        }
    });
```

```
Assert.AreEqual(source.Count, destination.Count);
```

This code will run without errors. However, its efficiency will be less than doing the same job from a single thread. Instead of doing calculations, a thread will be waiting for a shared resource (in this case, it is the destination variable) access. This situation is called thread **contention**, and it can significantly decrease your program performance.

To use all the available CPU cores effectively, we always have to try to reduce contention as much as possible. In some cases, it is possible to use special synchronization primitives or lock-free algorithms, or use thread local computations, which are merged at the end of parallel calculations to get the final result.

Implementing a cache with ReaderWriterLockSlim

Caching is a common technique that is being used in many applications to increase performance and efficiency. Usually, reading from a cache occurs more often than writing operation, and the number of cache readers is higher that the number of writers.

In this particular case, there is no sense in using an exclusive lock preventing other threads from reading another cache value. There is a built-in synchronization object that has exactly this behavior, and it is called ReaderWriterLockSlim.

There are several classes in the .NET Framework inside the System. Threading namespace, whose names end with Slim. It is usually more efficient and lightweight to implement the corresponding classes without Slim at the end of their names. In most cases, you should prefer the Slim versions over original ones, unless you are 100% sure why you need non-slim objects. This rule works with the ReaderWriterLock and ReaderWriterLockSlim classes as well—always prefer a Slim object, because it has major efficiency and corrective improvements.

Cache can be used differently in the application, but the most common approach is using **cache aside** pattern. The client is unaware of caching; if there is a long-running operation and no result of this operation can be found in the cache, we perform the operation and save the result into the cache. If there is a result in the cache, we do not start a long-running operation but use the cached value instead.

A simple code of a cache provider that contains one long-running operation and implements cache aside pattern will look as follows:

```
public class CustomProvider
{
    private readonly Dictionary<string, OperationResult> _cache =
        new Dictionary<string, OperationResult>();

    private readonly ReaderWriterLockSlim _rwLockSlim =
        new ReaderWriterLockSlim();

    public OperationResult RunOperationOrGetFromCache(
        string operationId)
    {
        _rwLockSlim.EnterReadLock();
        try
        {
            OperationResult result;
            if (_cache.TryGetValue(operationId, out result))
                return result;
        }
        finally
        {
            _rwLockSlim.ExitReadLock();
        }

        _rwLockSlim.EnterWriteLock();

        try
        {
            OperationResult result;
            if (_cache.TryGetValue(operationId, out result))
                return result;

            result = RunLongRunningOperation(operationId);
            _cache.Add(operationId, result);
            return result;
        }
        finally
        {
            _rwLockSlim.ExitReadLock();
        }
    }
```

```
private OperationResult RunLongRunningOperation(
    string operationId)
{
    // Running real long-running operation
    // ...
}
}
```

It is very important to always implement a cache invalidation strategy, which is missing in this demo code as it is not relevant to the topic of the chapter. However, in real-world scenarios, you have to pay attention to this to avoid memory leaks. The simple invalidation strategy can be setting a cache item lifetime explicitly or using weak references so that garbage collection will invalidate the cache.

This sample demonstrates a `CustomProvider` class, which contains only one `RunOperationOrGetFromCache` public method. This method accepts an operation identifier and returns the operation result as an `OperationResult` object. To implement correct cache parallel reading, in the beginning we acquire a reader lock and then check that there is a result in the cache. If not, we acquire a writer lock and then check that there is an operation value inside the cache, which can appear while we are acquiring the lock. If there is still nothing in the cache, we will run the long-running operation, put its result into the cache, and return it to the client.

If we don't perform this check, we can get `ArgumentException` when trying to add an item with the same key to the dictionary twice, and as a result we do unnecessary work.

However, as it usually happens in concurrent programming, this approach can be non-effective in different situations. Using `ReaderWriterLockSlim` for implementing dictionary-based caching almost always lead to worse performance than simply using a common statement, `lock (syncRoot)`. The problem is that acquiring reader lock is not a very fast operation. A `ReaderWriterLockSlim` object has to ensure that acquiring a writer lock is not possible while being inside a reader block, and this requires the use of some synchronization logic, which is costly. If a long running operation is really long running, this overhead is not significant. However, in our case, reading a value from `Dictionary` is a very fast operation, and in this situation, locking the overhead becomes noticeable. Since a lock statement uses spin-wait optimization for short running operations, it will be more effective in this particular case.

The previous tip works for choosing a data structure as well. In simple cases, implementing general locking over nonthread safe object could work better than a specialized universal thread safe data structure. However, when concurrent program logic becomes more complicated, it is a good idea to go for standard concurrent data structures.

Concurrent collections in .NET

Since the first .NET Framework version, most of the collections in the `System.Collections` namespace contained the `Synchronized` factory method that creates a thread safe wrapper over the collection instance, which ensures thread safety:

```
var source = Enumerable.Range(1, 42000).ToList();
var destination = ArrayList.Synchronized(new List<int>());

Parallel.ForEach(source,
    n =>
    {
        destination.Add(n);
    });

Assert.AreEqual(source.Count, destination.Count);
```

The synchronized collection wrapper can be used in a concurrent environment, but its efficiency is low, since it uses simple locking ensuring exclusive collection access for every operation. This approach is called **coarse-grained** locking and it is described in *Chapter 3, Understanding Parallelism Granularity*. It does not scale well with an increase in the number of clients and the amount of data inside the collection.

A complicated, but an efficient, approach is to use **fine-grained** locking, so we can provide an exclusive access only to the parts of the collection that are in use. For example, if the underlying data storage is an array, we can create multiple locks that will cover the corresponding array parts. This approach requires determining the required lock first, but it will also allow a non-blocking access to the different parts of the array. This will use locks only when there is a concurrent access to the same data. In certain scenarios, the performance difference will be huge.

PLINQ uses exactly the same approach for parallel collections processing. There is a special mechanism called partitioning, which splits a collection in multiple segments. Each segment gets processed on a separate thread. A standard partitioner implementation resides inside the `System.Collections.Concurrent.Partitioner` type.

With the .NET Framework 4.0 release, a new set of concurrent collections are available for .NET developers. These collections are specifically designed for high load concurrent access and use lock-free and fine-grained approaches internally. These collections are available in the `System.Collections.Concurrent` namespace:

Concurrent Collection	System.Collections.Generic analogue
ConcurrentDictionary<TKey, TValue>	Dictionary<TKey, TValue>
ConcurrentBag<T>	None
ConcurrentQueue<T>	Queue<T>
ConcurrentStack<T>	Stack<T>

Each of these concurrent collections are suitable for different work scenarios. Further, we will go through all of these data structures and review the implementation details and the best-suited work scenario.

ConcurrentDictionary

We can improve the implementation of `CustomProvider` using `ConcurrentDictionary<TKey, TValue>` to handle the synchronization:

```
public class CustomProvider
{
    private readonly
        ConcurrentDictionary<string, OperationResult> _cache =
            new ConcurrentDictionary<string, OperationResult>();

    public OperationResult RunOperationOrGetFromCache(
        string operationId)
    {
        return _cache.GetOrAdd(operationId,
            id => RunLongRunningOperation(id));
    }

    private OperationResult RunLongRunningOperation(
        string operationId)
    {
```

```
        // Running real long-running operation
        // ...
        Console.WriteLine("Running long-running operation");
        return OperationResult.Create(operationId);
    }
}
```

The code became much simpler. We just used the GetOrAdd method and it does exactly what we need; if there is an element in the dictionary, it just returns its value or runs a provided delegate, gets the result value, and stores it in the dictionary.

Every concurrent collection implements a corresponding generic interface. For example, ConcurrentDictionary<TKey, TValue> implements the standard IDictionary<TKey, TValue> interface. However besides this, it introduces new methods because it is not enough to introduce the thread safe version of each method. Consider this example:

```
private readonly IDictionary<string, OperationResult> _cache =
    new ConcurrentDictionary<string, OperationResult>();

public OperationResult RunOperationOrGetFromCache(
    string operationId)
{
    OperationResult result;

    if (_cache.TryGetValue(operationId, out result))
    {
        return result;
    }

    result = RunLongRunningOperation(operationId);
    _cache.Add(operationId, result);
    return result;
}
```

This code will not work correctly in a multithreaded environment. Both the TryGetValue and Add operations are thread safe, but a sequence of two operations without additional synchronization can cause a race condition, and in this example, it is possible to get an exception thrown from the Add method while trying to add an element when it has already been added to the dictionary by another thread.

It is clear that in this situation, just having the `IDictionary<TKey, TValue>` implementation is not enough. One of the possible solutions is to replace `_cache.Add` with the `_cache.TryAdd` method, but this will require us to get back to using a concrete class:

```
private readonly
    ConcurrentDictionary<string, OperationResult> _cache =
        new ConcurrentDictionary<string, OperationResult>();

public OperationResult RunOperationOrGetFromCache(
    string operationId)
{
    OperationResult result;
    if (_cache.TryGetValue(operationId, out result))
    {
        return result;
    }

    result = RunLongRunningOperation(operationId);
    _cache.TryAdd(operationId, result);
    return result;
}
```

While this solution is also far from perfect, we can already see why concurrent collections changed the common API and introduced a set of new methods. Usually, these new methods represent atomic operations that consist of several steps and each step performs a specific action internally: `GetOrAdd`, `AddOrUpdate`, and so on.

Now let's review one more important aspect of this implementation. If we look at the code thoroughly, we can see that despite there being no errors in the concurrent environment it is possible that the `RunLongRunningOperation` method can be called twice. Thus, only the first result will be stored in the dictionary and the latter method call result will be wasted. This is also important because the `GetOrAdd` method of the `ConcurrentDictionary<TKey, TValue>` class is implemented in a very similar way.

This means that using `RunOperationOrGetFromCache` in a concurrent environment will result in calling a long running operation multiple times per one value. If this turns out to be costly, similar to transmitting a large volume of data via the network or performing CPU intensive long time calculations, this is definitely not a good approach.

Using Lazy<T>

Since `AddOrGet` is implemented in a way that every call to this method with the same key will result in getting the same value, we can use a little trick to prevent the long running operation from running multiple times:

```
private readonly
    ConcurrentDictionary<string, Lazy<OperationResult>> _cache =
        new ConcurrentDictionary<string, Lazy<OperationResult>>();

public OperationResult RunOperationOrGetFromCache(
    string operationId)
{
    return _cache.GetOrAdd(operationId,
        id => new Lazy<OperationResult>(
            () => RunLongRunningOperation(id))).Value;
}
```

In this example, we wrap the `RunLongRunningOperation` method call into a special object—`Lazy<OperationResult>`. This class is a part of the .NET Framework Base Class Library (BCL) that ensures that the provided delegate will be executed only once and only when its `Value` property is accessed by an external code.

We can look at the `GetOrAdd` method implementation details to fully understand what is happening under the hood:

```
// ConcurrentDictionary<TKey, TValue> implementation
public TValue GetOrAdd(TKey key, Func<TKey, TValue> valueFactory)
{
    TValue resultingValue;
    if (TryGetValue(key, out resultingValue))
    {
        return resultingValue;
    }

    TryAddInternal(key, valueFactory(key), false, true,
        out resultingValue);

    return resultingValue;
}

/// <summary>
/// Shared internal implementation for inserts and updates.
/// If key exists, we always return false;
/// and if updateIfExists == true we
```

```
/// force update with value;
/// If key doesn't exist, we always add value and return true;
/// </summary>
private bool TryAddInternal(TKey key, TValue value,
    bool updateIfExists, bool acquireLock,
    out TValue resultingValue)
{
    // ... The implementation details
}
```

.NET Framework Core is now open source and can be found on GitHub in the Microsoft/dotnet repository. However, there is a more convenient way to learn the .NET source code—a referencesource.microsoft.com web site. This resource was specifically created for learning the internals of .NET and provides a comfortable search and navigation using the code semantics, not just a simple text search. For example, if you are looking for all the cases of the `System.String.Substring(System.Int32)` method usage, you will not get any other `Substring` method overloads.

We can see that if there is no cached operation result in the dictionary, we immediately call `valueFactory(key)` (this is where multiple `RunLongRunningOperation` calls happen), and the returned result goes to the `TryAddInternal` method. Even the comments to this method state that if a key exists and the `updateIfExists` parameter equals to `false`, we will use the old value that has been already stored in the dictionary.

Using `Lazy<OperationResult>` instead of `OperationResult` leads to a situation where we call only the `Lazy<T>` object constructor multiple times, while a long running operation will be executed only once when the first `GetOrAdd` method call completes.

Implementation details

`ConcurrentDictionary` is in fact a usual hash table that contains an array of buckets protected by an array of locks. The number of locks can be defined by the user and theoretically, allows many threads to access the dictionary without any contention if they all use different locks and thus, the different parts of data in the dictionary.

A `ConcurrentDictionary` inner structure scheme looks like this:

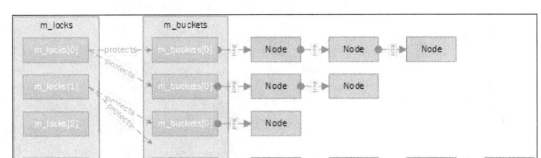

The entire `ConcurrentDictionary` state is placed in a separate `Tables` class instance in the `m_tables` field. This makes it possible to have an atomic state change operation for the dictionary with the help of the **compare-and-swap** (CAS) operations.

The `Tables` class contains the following most important fields:

- `m_buckets`: This is an array of buckets; each of the buckets contains a singly-linked list of nodes with dictionary data.

- `m_locks`: This is an array of locks; each lock provides synchronized access to one or more buckets.

- `m_countPerLock`: This is an array of counters; each counter contains a total number of nodes that are protected by the corresponding lock. For example, if we look at the previous scheme, where the first lock protects the first two buckets, the `m_countPerLock[0]` element will contain the value of 5.

- `m_comparer`: This is an `IEqualityComparer<TKey>` object that contains the logic for calculating the hash value of a key object.

The `ConcurrentDictionary` class in turn contains three large operations groups:

- **Lock-free** operations: This kind of operation can be run in parallel from multiple threads without any contention

- **Fine-grained lock** operations: As it has been already explained, these operations can be concurrently executed without any contention if they manipulate the different parts of data inside the dictionary

- **Exclusive lock** operations: These operations can run only on a single thread and require a full collection lock to ensure thread safety

Lock-free operations

These operations do not require any lock and can be used safely from multiple threads. This is the list of the corresponding methods:

- `ContainsKey`
- `TryGetValue`
- Read access by dictionary indexer
- `GetEnumerator`

The first three operations are based on the `TryGetValue` method. This contains the following steps:

1. Get the key object hash code using current comparer.
2. Get the bucket number by the key hash with the help of the `GetBucketAndLockNo` method. The lock number is not used at the moment.
3. Iterate over the current bucket node list to find the corresponding value:

```
public bool TryGetValue(TKey key, out TValue value)
{
    int bucketNo, lockNoUnused;

    Tables tables = m_tables;
    GetBucketAndLockNo(
        tables.m_comparer.GetHashCode(key), out bucketNo, out
lockNoUnused,
        tables.m_buckets.Length, tables.m_locks.Length);

    // The Volatile.Read ensures that the load of the
    // fields of 'n' doesn't move before the load from buckets[i].
    Node n = Volatile.Read<Node>(ref tables.m_buckets[bucketNo]);

    // Iterate over Nodes to find entry with a corresponding key
    ...
}
```

The `GetEnumerator` method implementation is quite straightforward:

```
public IEnumerator<KeyValuePair<TKey, TValue>> GetEnumerator()
{
    Node[] buckets = m_tables.m_buckets;

    for (int i = 0; i < buckets.Length; i++)
    {
```

```
    // The Volatile.Read ensures that
    // the load of the fields of 'current'
    // doesn't move before the load from buckets[i].
    Node current = Volatile.Read<Node>(ref buckets[i]);

    while (current != null)
    {
        yield return new KeyValuePair<TKey, TValue>(
            current.m_key, current.m_value);

        current = current.m_next;
    }
}
}
```

As we can see, the `GetEnumerator` method does not create a copy of buckets contents, and this allows multiple threads to change the dictionary data while another thread iterates over these elements. Notice the `Volatile.Read` construct that creates an acquire-fence and ensures that no reads or writes can be reordered before the load from `buckets[i]`.

Fine-grained lock operations

These operations usually work with a single element inside the dictionary. These methods use the fine-grained locking approach:

- `TryAdd`
- `TryRemove`
- `TryUpdate`
- write access by a dictionary indexer
- `GetOrAdd`
- `AddOrUpdate`

These operations internally use the `GetBucketAndLockNo` method, which returns the bucket and the lock numbers. The implementation usually contains the following steps:

1. Get the key object hash code.
2. Get the bucket and the lock numbers.
3. Acquire the lock.

4. Change the current bucket—delete or change some element inside.

5. Release the acquired lock.

Most of the operations in the preceding list use the `TryAddInternal` method internally. Let's review the simplified code of this method:

```
private bool TryAddInternal(TKey key, TValue value,
    out TValue resultingValue)
{
    while (true)
    {
        bool resizeDesired = false;
        var tables = m_tables;
        int bucketNo, lockNo;
        int hashcode = tables.m_comparer.GetHashCode(key);

        GetBucketAndLockNo(hashcode, out bucketNo, out lockNo);

        try
        {
            Monitor.Enter(tables.m_locks[lockNo]);

            // If the table just got resized, we may not be holding
            // the right lock, and must retry.
            // This should be a rare occurence.
            if (tables != m_tables)
            {
                continue;
            }

            // Looping through Nodes in the bucket.
            // If existing Node was found
            // the method returns false, otherwise
            // new Node would be added
            for (Node node = tables.m_buckets[bucketNo];
                    node != null; node = node.m_next)
            {
                // ...
            }

            // If the number of elements guarded by this lock has
            // exceeded the budget, resize the bucket table.
            // It is also possible that GrowTable will increase
            // the budget but won't resize the bucket table.
```

```
                    // That happens if the bucket table is found to be
                    // poorly utilized due to a bad hash function.
                    if (tables.m_countPerLock[lockNo] > m_budget)
                    {
                        resizeDesired = true;
                    }
                }
                finally
                {
                    Monitor.Exit(tables.m_locks[lockNo]);
                }

                // Resize table if needed.
                // This method should be called outside the lock
                // to prevent a deadlocks.
                if (resizeDesired)
                {
                    GrowTable(tables, tables.m_comparer);
                }

                resultingValue = value;
                return true;
            }
        }
```

It is clear that this code implements all the preceding steps — we get the key hash, the bucket, and the lock number and proceed to the element needed. However, there are a couple of important points to pay attention to:

- Using the **while** loop to work around the situation where another thread has changed the collection and its `m_tables` field. In this case, we just retry until we succeed and the old and new `m_tables` values remain equal.

- When node count per one lock exceeds some threshold value (`m_budget`), the hash table rebalancing occurs inside the `GrowTable` method. This requires an exclusive lock for the dictionary to be acquired.

Exclusive lock operations

There are more operations that are required to get an exclusive lock as the `GrowTable` does. It is very important to know these operations and avoid using them in a multithreaded environment if possible. Here is the operations list:

- `Clear`
- `ToArray`

- CopyTo
- Count
- IsEmpty
- GetKeys
- GetValues

We remember that trying to work with multiple locks can easily lead to deadlocks in a concurrent program. Fortunately, the concurrent dictionary contains the AcquireLocks method that can safely acquire multiple locks always in the same order that prevents deadlocks. This method is used internally from the AcquireAllLocks method, which safely acquires all the locks in the dictionary.

Every operation listed previously uses the same algorithm; first, it calls AcquireAllLocks to prevent concurrent changes to the dictionary, then it modifies the m_table instance and changes the dictionary state. For example, here is how the Count property is implemented:

```
public int Count
{
    get
    {
        int count = 0;

        try
        {
            // Acquire all locks
            AcquireAllLocks();

            // Compute the count, we allow overflow
            for (int i = 0; i < m_tables.m_countPerLock.Length; i++)
            {
                count += m_tables.m_countPerLock[i];
            }

        }
        finally
        {
            // Release locks that have been acquired earlier
            ReleaseLocks();
        }

        return count;
    }
}
```

Using the implementation details in practice

Knowing the principles of how the concurrent dictionary is implemented can help you in some practical situations.

A better understanding of concurrent dictionary constructor parameters, for example, `concurrencyLevel`, will help to tune up your data structure for the concrete task. On one hand, the more locks we create, the more threads can potentially work with the dictionary without locking, which is a good thing. On the other hand, creating more locks creates more performance overhead, and we cannot explicitly set a lock control or a bucket, so this can lead to decline of performance. Knowing these details will help us to study the program under a profiler to find the best solution for our concrete case.

Another important implementation aspect is the dictionary buckets containing singly-linked lists. Adding an element to such a list is an O(N) operation and this can be a problem when storing hundreds of thousands of small items in the dictionary.

Since the `Count`, `ToArray`, and `IsEmpty` operations require exclusive locking, in some cases using corresponding LINQ alternatives such as `Enumerable.Count()`, `Enumerable.ToArray()`, and `Enumerable.Any()` will be much more efficient in situations where the dictionary often gets concurrently updated.

ConcurrentBag<T>

`ConcurrentBag<T>` is one of the simplest concurrent collections. It is intended to store any general-purpose data. The main feature of this collection is how it stores the data; the `Add` method appends an item to a doubly-linked list that is stored in the current thread's local storage. This makes the appending operation very efficient, since there is no contention. Getting an item from the collection with the `TryTake` or `TryPeek` methods is also quite efficient. First, we look for the item in the local list, but if it is empty, we look for items in other threads' local lists.

This approach is called **work stealing** and works well when each thread contains more or less the same number of data and uses the same number of append and take operations.

Let's review an example of using the `ConcurrentBag<T>` data structure:

```
var bag = new ConcurrentBag<string>();

var task1 = Run(() =>
{
    AddAndPrint(bag, "[T1]: Item 1");
    AddAndPrint(bag, "[T1]: Item 2");
```

```
        AddAndPrint(bag, "[T1]: Item 3");

        Thread.Sleep(2000);
        TakeAndPrint(bag);
        TakeAndPrint(bag);
    }, threadName: "T1");

    var task2 = Run(() =>
    {
        AddAndPrint(bag, "[T2]: Item 1");
        AddAndPrint(bag, "[T2]: Item 2");
        AddAndPrint(bag, "[T2]: Item 3");

        Thread.Sleep(1000);
        TakeAndPrint(bag);
        TakeAndPrint(bag);
        TakeAndPrint(bag);
        TakeAndPrint(bag);
    }, threadName: "T2");

    Task.WaitAll(task1, task2);
```

The `AddAndPrint`, `TakeAndPrint` and `Run` methods help to create a thread with a given name and allows us to append and remove elements from the `ConcurrentBag<T>` object, while printing the element value to the console:

```
    private static Task Run(Action action, string threadName)
    {
        var tcs = new TaskCompletionSource<object>();
        var thread = new Thread(() =>
        {
            action();
            tcs.SetResult(null);
        });
        thread.Name = threadName;
        thread.Start();

        return tcs.Task;
    }

    private static void AddAndPrint(ConcurrentBag<string> bag,
        string value)
    {
        Console.WriteLine("{0}: Add - {1}",
            Thread.CurrentThread.Name, value);
```

```
        bag.Add(value);
}

private static void TakeAndPrint(ConcurrentBag<string> bag)
{
    string value;
    if (bag.TryTake(out value))
    {
        Console.WriteLine("{0}: Take - {1}",
            Thread.CurrentThread.Name, value);
    }
}
```

Here we created two tasks, and each task sets two elements to the queue. Then it waits for some time and starts to process the appended elements. The inner storage structure of the ConcurrentBag object will look like this when the appending of the elements is finished:

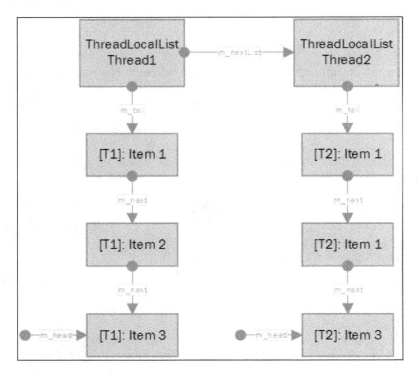

`ConcurrentBag<T>`, as we have already mentioned, contains several doubly-linked lists, one list for each thread. Adding an item leads to appending it to the end of the local list, but getting items from the concurrent bag is slightly more complicated:

```
T2: Add  - [T2]: Item 1
T1: Add  - [T1]: Item 1
T2: Add  - [T2]: Item 2
T2: Add  - [T2]: Item 3
T1: Add  - [T1]: Item 2
T1: Add  - [T1]: Item 3
T2: Take - [T2]: Item 3
T2: Take - [T2]: Item 2
T2: Take - [T2]: Item 1
T2: Take - [T1]: Item 1
T1: Take - [T1]: Item 3
T1: Take - [T1]: Item 2
```

We append items to the collection from two threads, and this explains an addition order that was demonstrated previously. The most interesting thing is how items are removed from `ConcurrentBag`. In our case, the second thread starts getting the items from the collection. First, it gets the elements that were added by this thread, but in the reverse order (from the end of the doubly-linked list). When the local list becomes empty, it tries to "steal" work from another thread, but this time it gets items from the beginning of the underlying list.

ConcurrentBag in practice

The implementation details of the `ConcurrentBag<T>` data structure makes it useful only in very specific scenarios. Reading and writing objects has to happen on the same thread to minimize contention. It makes this collection not very useful in most common situations, since usually different threads append and read data from a collection.

A good practical scenario for `ConcurrentBag<T>` is an object pool. It is usually implemented in a way that when some object, which is significantly expensive to create, does not get cleaned up by the garbage collector, it goes to some object storage and is easily accessed when needed. Since usually such operations happen on a single thread, this will make a perfect condition to use this kind of concurrent collection.

Another similar example is a thread pool implementation. If we look closely at the `DefaultTaskScheduler` implementation from Task Parallel Library, we can see that it has the same behavior as the concurrent bag. This task scheduler does not use a global task list; instead, it creates a number of local task lists for each worker thread. If some task creates a child task (without providing the `PreferFairness` option), it will be appended to the local task list. This helps to reduce contention and has a higher probability of finding the required data in the CPU cache. Also it uses work stealing in case the local task list is empty.

However, even if the concurrent bag perfectly fits in your scenario, it is a good idea to try to use other data structures and measure and compare the performance of each implementation. The synthetic tests (they can be found in the code samples of this chapter) show that the `ConcurrentBag<T>` performance is not impressive, and maybe choosing `ConcurrentQueue<T>` or `ConcurrentStack<T>` will be a better solution. Even in perfect conditions when the same thread appends and retrieves data, a concurrent bag is about three times slower than a concurrent queue.

ConcurrentQueue<T>

`ConcurrentQueue<T>` is a concurrent version of the `Queue<T>` class. It contains three basic methods: `Enqueue` appends an item to the queue, `TryDequeue` retrieves an item from the queue if it is possible, and `TryPeek` gets the first element in the queue without removing it from the queue. The last two methods return false if the queue is empty.

Now let's see a sample code for `ConcurrentQueue<T>`:

```
var queue = new ConcurrentQueue<string>();

var task1 = Run(() =>
{
    AddAndPrint(queue, "[T1]: Item 1");
    AddAndPrint(queue, "[T1]: Item 2");
    AddAndPrint(queue, "[T1]: Item 3");

    Thread.Sleep(2000);
    TakeAndPrint(queue);
    TakeAndPrint(queue);
}, threadName: "T1");

var task2 = Run(() =>
{
    AddAndPrint(queue, "[T2]: Item 1");
    AddAndPrint(queue, "[T2]: Item 2");
```

```
        AddAndPrint(queue, "[T2]: Item 3");

        Thread.Sleep(1000);
        TakeAndPrint(queue);
        TakeAndPrint(queue);
        TakeAndPrint(queue);
        TakeAndPrint(queue);
    }, threadName: "T2");

    Task.WaitAll(task1, task2);
```

In this example, we do the same with the ConcurrentBag<T> code. We create two named threads; each thread appends three items to the queue. Then after some pause, threads start to retrieve the elements from the queue:

```
T1: Add - [T1]: Item 1
T2: Add - [T2]: Item 1
T2: Add - [T2]: Item 2
T2: Add - [T2]: Item 3
T1: Add - [T1]: Item 2
T1: Add - [T1]: Item 3
T2: Dequeue - [T1]: Item 1
T2: Dequeue - [T2]: Item 1
T2: Dequeue - [T2]: Item 2
T2: Dequeue - [T2]: Item 3
T1: Dequeue - [T1]: Item 2
T1: Dequeue - [T1]: Item 3
```

Concurrent queue is a FIFO (First In, First Out) collection, but since this is a multithreaded environment, the order of appending and removing elements is not strictly sequential.

The ConcurrentQueue<T> class is implemented on a singly-linked list of ring buffers (or segments). This allows this collection to be lock-free that makes it very attractive to use this in high load concurrent applications.

In the beginning, a concurrent queue creates one segment that is referenced by two inner fields: m_head and m_tail (the first and the last segments reference correspondingly). The segment size is 32 bytes, and each segment contains two references: Low and High. Low references an element position in the buffer that can be removed by calling the Dequeue method, and High references the last item in the buffer that has been added by using the Enqueue method.

Here is how the queue will look internally after appending six elements and then removing two of them:

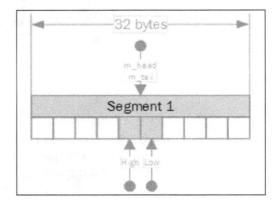

If we find out during the process of appending an element to the queue that the segment is full, then one more segment is created and attached to the end of the segment list. Only the first and the last segments can be partially full, every other segment must be completely full.

If we append 80 elements and then remove four, we will see something like this:

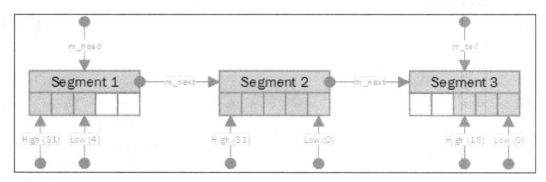

The overall queue size will be *32 – 4 + 32 + 16 = 76*. The queue will contain three segments, and the first and the last segments will be partially filled.

ConcurrentStack<T>

The ConcurrentStack<T> data structure is a concurrent version of a standard Stack<T> collection. It contains three main methods: Push, TryPop, and TryPeek, to append, retrieve and get the item from the collection by FILO (First In, Last Out) principle.

ConcurrentStack<T> is implemented as a singly-linked lock-free list, which makes it less interesting in terms of reviewing the implementation details. Nevertheless, it is still useful to know, and if we have to choose a concurrent data structure for a scenario where elements processing order is not important, it is preferable to use a concurrent queue since it has less performance overhead. Appending elements to the concurrent stack always leads to additional memory allocation, which can be a significant drawback in certain scenarios.

The Producer/Consumer pattern

The Producer/Consumer pattern is one of the most widely used parallel programming patterns. The most natural approach is to organize your application for processing work items on another thread. In this case, we get two application parts—one puts new work to be processed and the other checks for new work and performs element processing. The standard .NET Framework thread pool is a good example; one thread puts a work item in a processing queue by calling the Task.Run function of the ThreadPool.QueueUserWorkItem methods, and the infrastructure finds other threads to process these tasks.

> The other parallel programming patterns will be reviewed in the next chapter. The Producer/Consumer pattern is very tightly related to concurrent data structures, and it is more naturally described along with them.

Another classic example is a user interface programming. To create responsive and fast UI, a UI thread has to offload as much work as possible to other threads. Therefore, it posts tasks to a queue, and some background threads process these tasks and provide the result back to UI.

The same approach is used in server-side programming. To effectively process client requests, they are queued first, and only then does the server infrastructure assign a worker thread to process the user request.

Custom Producer/Consumer pattern implementation

Let's try to implement the Producer/Consumer pattern with the help of the standard Queue<T> class. Before we can get to the programming, we have to think about the requirements:

- What should a consumer do when calling the Take method while the current queue does not contain any elements?

- What should a producer do when calling the Add method as the collection size has reached some threshold value?

If we look at the standard concurrent collections implementation, it makes sense to replace the Take method with TryTake, and this will return **false** if the queue is empty. Instead of the Add method, we can implement TryAdd that will return **false** when the queue is full. Unfortunately, it is not the best design for a Producer/Consumer queue.

A more natural approach would be to make the Take method block the current thread when the underlying queue is empty and return the result as soon as any producer thread adds an item to the queue; such a queue is called a **blocking queue**. The same with the Add method—just block when the queue is full and put an item as soon as there is a place for an item in the queue. This approach helps us to handle a situation when there are too many producers or they just create more items that consumers can handle. This kind of queue is called a **bounded queue**.

A simple BoundedBlockingQueue implementation will look like this:

```
public class BoundedBlockingQueue<T>
{
    private readonly Queue<T> _queue = new Queue<T>();

    private readonly SemaphoreSlim _nonEmptyQueueSemaphore =
        new SemaphoreSlim(0, int.MaxValue);


    private readonly SemaphoreSlim _nonFullQueueSemaphore;

    public BoundedBlockingQueue(int boundedCapacity)
    {
        _nonFullQueueSemaphore = new SemaphoreSlim(
            boundedCapacity);
    }
```

```
public void Add(T value)
{
    _nonFullQueueSemaphore.Wait();

    lock (_queue) _queue.Enqueue(value);
    _nonEmptyQueueSemaphore.Release();
}

public T Take()
{
    _nonEmptyQueueSemaphore.Wait();
    T result;
    lock (_queue)
    {
        Debug.Assert(_queue.Count != 0);
        result = _queue.Dequeue();
    }

    _nonFullQueueSemaphore.Release();
    return result;
}
}
```

This implementation uses a simple queue and two semaphores — _nonFullQueueSemaphore and _nonEmptyQueueSemaphore. We use the first one to block producers when the queue is full; the second blocks consumers when the queue is empty. When the Add method is called; we call Wait on _nonFullQueueSemaphore. It will return control when the queue is not full, and then we can add another semaphore counter to unblock consumer threads. The Take method works exactly like this, but in a reverse order — we wait on the _nonEmptyQueueSemaphore semaphore until we have anything in the queue, and then we remove the appeared element from the queue and increase the other semaphore counter.

> In the production code, we will have to implement IDisposable to support deterministic resources releasing, proper exception handling, and cancellation policy by providing the CancellationToken instance to the Add and Take methods. However, in this example, it is not relevant to the topic and this logic is omitted to keep the remaining code clean and simple.

In some cases, the Producer/Consumer queue can be used to process a fixed (or at least a finite) number of elements. In this case, we need to be able to notify the consumers that items appending is over:

```
public class BoundedBlockingQueue<T>
{
    private readonly Queue<T> _queue = new Queue<T>();

    private readonly SemaphoreSlim _nonEmptyQueueSemaphore =
        new SemaphoreSlim(0, int.MaxValue);

    private readonly
        CancellationTokenSource _consumersCancellationTokenSource =
            new CancellationTokenSource();

    private readonly SemaphoreSlim _nonFullQueueSemaphore;

    public BoundedBlockingQueue(int boundedCapacity)
    {
        _nonFullQueueSemaphore = new SemaphoreSlim(boundedCapacity);
    }

    public void CompleteAdding()
    {
        // Notify all the consumers that completion is finished
        _consumersCancellationTokenSource.Cancel();
    }

    public void Add(T value)
    {
        _nonFullQueueSemaphore.Wait();

        lock (_queue) _queue.Enqueue(value);
        _nonEmptyQueueSemaphore.Release();
    }

    public T Take()
    {
        T item;
        if (!TryTake(out item))
        {
            throw new InvalidOperationException();
        }
```

```
        return item;
    }

    public IEnumerable<T> Consume()
    {
        T element;

        while(TryTake(out element))
        {
            yield return element;
        }
    }

    private bool TryTake(out T result)
    {
        result = default(T);

        if (!_nonEmptyQueueSemaphore.Wait(0))
        {
            try
            {
                _nonEmptyQueueSemaphore.Wait(
                    _consumersCancellationTokenSource.Token);
            }
            catch (OperationCanceledException e)
            {
                // Breaking the loop only when cancellation
                // was requested by CompleteAdding
                if (e.CancellationToken ==
                        _consumersCancellationTokenSource.Token)
                {
                    return false;
                }

                // Propagate original exception
                throw;
            }
        }

        lock (_queue)
        {
            result = _queue.Dequeue();
        }
```

```
            _nonFullQueueSemaphore.Release();
            return true;
        }
    }
```

Here we see new `CompleteAdding` and `Consume` methods. The first one is intended to be used from producer's code to signal that we have finished appending items to the queue. The `Consume` method can be used by consumers to process all the items until the queue is empty and item appending is complete.

We have also implemented a cooperative cancellation here with the help of the `CancellationTokenSource` and `CancellationToken` objects. The `CompleteAdding` method sets the flag that indicates that no additional elements will be added to the collection. The `TryTake` method uses this flag and standard semaphore cancellation logic to break the loop when cancellation is requested.

We can use our brand new collection in the following way:

```
var queue = new BoundedBlockingQueue<string>(3);

var t1 = Task.Run(() =>
{
    AddAndPrint(queue, "1");
    AddAndPrint(queue, "2");
    AddAndPrint(queue, "3");
    AddAndPrint(queue, "4");
    AddAndPrint(queue, "5");

    queue.CompleteAdding();
    Console.WriteLine("[{0}]: finished producing elements",
        Thread.CurrentThread.ManagedThreadId);

});

var t2 = Task.Run(() =>
{
    foreach (var element in queue.Consume())
    {
        Print(element);
    }

    Console.WriteLine("[{0}]: Processing finished.",
        Thread.CurrentThread.ManagedThreadId);
});
```

```
var t3 = Task.Run(() =>
{
    foreach (var element in queue.Consume())
    {
        Print(element);
    }

    Console.WriteLine("[{0}]: Processing finished.",
        Thread.CurrentThread.ManagedThreadId);
});

Task.WaitAll(t1, t2, t3);
```

In this code, we used one producer thread that appends items to the queue, and two consumer threads. The result will be the following:

```
[4]: Added 1
[9]: Took 1
[8]: Took 2
[4]: Added 2
[4]: Added 3
[4]: Added 4
[4]: Added 5
[9]: Took 3
[9]: Took 5
[4]: finished producing elements
[8]: Took 4
[9]: Processing finished.
[8]: Processing finished.
```

The Producer/Consumer pattern in .NET 4.0+

Since .NET Framework 4.0, there has been a standard `BlockingCollection<T>` class, so we should prefer using this to create our own implementations such as `BoundedBlockingQueue<T>`. It contains all the required operations and allows us to choose different element storage strategies using different concurrent collections.

In spite of `BlockingCollection<T>` implementing the `ICollection<T>` interface, it is just a wrapper over any general concurrent collection that implements `IProducerConsumerCollection<T>`. The `Blocking` part of the collection name means that the `Take` method blocks until new elements appear in the collection. A more accurate name for this collection would be `BoundedBlockingProducerConsumer<T>`, since it also blocks the `Add` method when the maximum underlying collection capacity is reached.

Let's use `BlockingCollection<T>` to create a custom Producer/Consumer implementation that allows us to create a specific number of consumer threads:

```
public class CustomProducerConsumer<T> : IDisposable
{
    private readonly Action<T> _consumeItem;
    private readonly BlockingCollection<T> _blockingCollection;
    private readonly Task[] _workers;

    public CustomProducerConsumer(Action<T> consumeItem,
        int degreeOfParallelism,
        int capacity = 1024)
    {
        _consumeItem = consumeItem;

        _blockingCollection = new BlockingCollection<T>(capacity);

        _workers = Enumerable.Range(1, degreeOfParallelism)
            .Select(_ => Task.Factory.StartNew(Worker,
                TaskCreationOptions.LongRunning))
            .ToArray();
    }

    public void Process(T item)
    {
        _blockingCollection.Add(item);
    }

    public void CompleteProcessing()
    {
        _blockingCollection.CompleteAdding();
    }

    public void Dispose()
    {
        // Unblock all workers even if the client
```

```
        // didn't call CompleteProcessing
        if (!_blockingCollection.IsAddingCompleted)
        {
            _blockingCollection.CompleteAdding();
        }

        Task.WaitAll(_workers);

        _blockingCollection.Dispose();
    }

    private void Worker()
    {
        foreach (var item in
            _blockingCollection.GetConsumingEnumerable())
        {
            _consumeItem(item);
        }
    }
}
```

The constructor of `CustomProducerConsumer<T>` accepts as a parameter an `Action<T>` delegate that represents the consumer, queue size, and required parallelism degree. Then, we create the required number of worker threads by creating the `Task` objects with the `TaskCreationOptions.LongRunning` option. The process method is intended to append new elements, and the `CompleteProcessing` method signals that there will be no more elements appended to the queue:

```
Action<string> processor = element =>
{
    Console.WriteLine("[{0}]: Processing element '{1}'",
        Thread.CurrentThread.ManagedThreadId, element);
};

var producerConcumer = new CustomProducerConsumer<string>(
    processor, Environment.ProcessorCount);

for (int i = 0; i < 5; i++)
{
    string item = "Item " + (i + 1);
    Console.WriteLine("[{0}]: Adding element '{1}'",
        Thread.CurrentThread.ManagedThreadId, item);

    producerConcumer.Process("Item " + (i + 1));
}
```

```
Console.WriteLine("[{0}]: Complete adding new elements",
    Thread.CurrentThread.ManagedThreadId);

producerConcumer.CompleteProcessing();

// Dispose will block till all operations gets completed
producerConcumer.Dispose();
```

If we run this code, we will get the following result:

```
[5]: Adding element 'Item 1'
[5]: Adding element 'Item 2'
[5]: Adding element 'Item 3'
[9]: Processing element 'Item 1'
[8]: Processing element 'Item 2'
[5]: Adding element 'Item 4'
[5]: Adding element 'Item 5'
[5]: Complete adding new elements
[9]: Processing element 'Item 5'
[10]: Processing element 'Item 3'
[11]: Processing element 'Item 4'
```

The result shows that there is one producer thread that appends elements to the collection, and four different consumer threads that process these elements until the producer thread stops appending items.

Summary

In this chapter, we have learned about different concurrent data structures, their advantages and disadvantages, and we have understood that choosing an appropriate concurrent data structure is a complicated and responsible task. The right choice is defined by many criteria such as availability, complexity, resource consumption, versatility, performance, and many others.

Similar to software development, in general there is no single and proper universal solution appropriate for all usage scenarios. In some cases, it is better to use regular collections with exclusive locking. Some other cases will require developing our own specific concurrent data structures from scratch, since a universal standard collection will not fit in the high performance requirements. A rule of thumb is to try to implement the easiest solution and then measure the performance and check where the performance bottleneck of your application is.

In the next chapter, we will consider different concurrent and asynchronous programming patterns that can help in structuring your parallel program for simplicity and efficiency and allow you to quickly implement well-known concurrent algorithms.

7
Leveraging Parallel Patterns

There are many programming rules, tricks, and typical patterns related to concurrent programming that have been developed to address concrete problems that often happen in practice. In this chapter, we will go through several kinds of concurrent programming patterns — low-level patterns (concurrent idioms), .NET-specific patterns for asynchronous programming (Asynchronous Programming Patterns), and high-level concurrent application building blocks (Concurrent Design Patterns). Let's review them one by one.

Concurrent idioms

The .NET Framework platform contains some high-level components that make concurrent applications programming much easier. In *Chapter 6*, *Using Concurrent Data Structures*, we reviewed concurrent collections and data structures, and in *Chapter 4*, *Task Parallel Library in Depth*, and *Chapter 5*, *C# Language Support for Asynchrony*, we looked at Task Parallel Library and the C# language `async`/`await` infrastructure.

Here, we will see how TPL and C# can improve your programming experience.

Process Tasks in Completion Order

As an example task, let's consider leveraging a weather information from a service for each provided city, processing the information, and printing it to the console. The simple implementation will be like this:

```
public async Task UpdateWeather()
{
  var cities = new List<string> { "Los Angeles", "Seattle",
    "New York" };
```

```
    var tasks =
      from city in cities
      select new { City = city, WeatherTask =
        GetWeatherForAsync(city) };

    foreach (var entry in tasks)
    {
      var weather = await entry.WeatherTask;

      ProcessWeather(entry.City, weather);
    }
  }

  private Task<Weather> GetWeatherForAsync(string city)
  {
    Console.WriteLine("Getting the weather for '{0}'", city);

    return WeatherService.GetWeatherAsync(city);
  }

  private void ProcessWeather(string city, Weather weather)
  {
    Console.WriteLine("[{2}]: Processing weather for '{0}': '{1}'",
      city, weather, DateTime.Now.ToLongTimeString());
  }
```

In this code, we used a LINQ query to get the weather data for each city. The program will work well, but there is a problem in this code; we call the weather info service one by one and a new request gets issued only after the preceding request has been completed. We can use a workaround by calling the ToList method on the query, but we will get the results in their starting order and not by task completion.

The solution is to use the Process Tasks in Completion Order idiom. The implementation is based on the Task.WhenAny method:

```
var cities = new List<string> { "Los Angeles", "Seattle",
  "New York" };
var tasks = cities.Select(async city =>
{
  return new {City = city, Weather = await
    GetWeatherForAsync(city)};
}).ToList();

while (tasks.Count != 0)
{
```

```
    var completedTask = await Task.WhenAny(tasks);

    tasks.Remove(completedTask);

    var result = completedTask.Result;

    ProcessWeather(result.City, result.Weather);
}
```

Here, we called the weather information service for all the cities in parallel, and then inside the **while** loop we used the `Task.WhenAny` method to get the first completed task. The task gets processed and removed from the running task list. As required in this example, tasks are being processed in completion order.

However, the code looks more complicated than the first sample. To get the code structured, we can create a generic `OrderByCompletion` implementation for the tasks collection:

```
public static IEnumerable<Task<T>> OrderByCompletion<T>(
   this IEnumerable<Task<T>> taskSequence)
{
    var tasks = taskSequence.ToList();

    while (tasks.Count != 0)
    {
      var tcs = new TaskCompletionSource<T>();

      // Getting the first finished task
      Task.WhenAny(tasks).ContinueWith((Task<Task<T>> tsk) => {
        tasks.Remove(tsk.Result);

        tcs.FromTask(tsk.Result);
      });

      yield return tcs.Task;
    }
}
```

Nevertheless, this implementation has a serious pitfall. Since the `Task.WhenAny` method creates a continuation task for each running task and we are calling it inside the loop, we can conclude that this `OrderByCompletion` method implementation has a time complexity of $O(n2)$. To improve the performance, we can register a continuation for each task that will use the `TaskCompletionSource` array to store each task's result.

It is very comfortable to use the newly implemented `OrderByCompletion` method:

```
var cities = new List<string> { "Los Angeles", "Seattle",
  "New York" };

var tasks = cities.Select(async city =>
{
  return new {City = city, Weather = await
    GetWeatherForAsync(city)};
});

foreach (var task in tasks.OrderByCompletion())
{
  var taskResult = await task;

  // taskResult is an object of anonymous type with City and
  // WeatherTask
    ProcessWeather(taskResult.City, taskResult.Weather);
}
```

Now it is possible to use the plain old `foreach` loop similarly to the first implementation, but the task processing happens by completion and not by start order. The results will demonstrate this processing behavior:

```
[12:54:35 PM]: Getting the weather for 'Los Angeles'

[12:54:35 PM]: Getting the weather for 'Seattle'

[12:54:35 PM]: Getting the weather for 'New York'

[12:54:36 PM]: Processing weather for 'Seattle': 'Temp: 7C'

Got the weather for 'Los Angeles'

[12:54:39 PM]: Processing weather for 'Los Angeles': 'Temp: 6C'

Got the weather for 'New York'

[12:54:40 PM]: Processing weather for 'New York': 'Temp: 8C'
```

Limiting the parallelism degree

To use computer resources effectively, we need to be able to specify the number of simultaneously running operations. Besides this, the optimal parallel operations number is related to their nature. If these operations are long-running and CPU-bound, it makes sense to use the number of hardware-supported threads to limit the parallelism degree.

However, if they are IO-bound, there is no clear limit. It depends on many factors related to the kind of IO that is happening and the corresponding hardware characteristics. It may be HDD random read speed, or network throughput and latency, or in the case of remote service calls, the performance of this service, and so on. Creating a general solution in this case is very hard and can be more complicated than creating our own implementation of a thread pool, which does the same for CPU-bound tasks.

However, for starters, we can just run multiple parallel operations and limit the parallelism degree with a certain number. Let's pretend that we did experiments with our weather info service and found out by measurements that the most effective option is to run only two simultaneous requests to this service.

One of the ways of implementing such a limit is by creating a `ForEachAsync` extension method that accept a `degreeOfParallelism` parameter:

```
public static IEnumerable<Task<TTask>>
  ForEachAsync<TItem, TTask>(
    this IEnumerable<TItem> source,
    Func<TItem, Task<TTask>> selector,
    int degreeOfParallelism)
    {

    // We need to know all the items in the source
    // before starting tasks
    var tasks = source.ToList();

    int completedTask = -1;

    // Creating an array of TaskCompletionSource that would hold
    // the results for each operations
    var taskCompletions = new
      TaskCompletionSource<TTask>[tasks.Count];

    for(int n = 0; n < taskCompletions.Length; n++)
        taskCompletions[n] = new TaskCompletionSource<TTask>();

    // Partitioner would do all grunt work for us and split
    // the source into appropriate number of chunks
    // for parallel processing
    foreach (var partition in Partitioner.Create(tasks).
      GetPartitions(degreeOfParallelism)) {
        var p = partition;
```

```
            // Loosing sync context and starting asynchronous
            // computation for each partition
        Task.Run(async () =>
        {
          while (p.MoveNext())
          {
                var task = selector(p.Current);

                // Don't want to use empty catch .
                // This trick just swallows an exception
                await task.ContinueWith(_ => { });

                int finishedTaskIndex = Interlocked.Increment(
                  ref completedTask);

                 taskCompletions[finishedTaskIndex]
                .FromTask(task);
          }
        });
        }

    return taskCompletions.Select(tcs => tcs.Task);
    }
```

There are several options that we can choose to implement a limit on the degree of parallelism. For example, we can use semaphores or other synchronization primitives. However, we can choose more comfortable options to use Task Parallel Library and its `Partitioner` type to get a set of partitions with the `Partitioner.CreatePartitioner` method call. Each of these partitions represents something like an iterator that can be used in parallel with other partitions. To store the completed tasks, we will use an array of `TaskCompletionSource` objects, which will hold the results in completion order.

The way of using this method is shown in the following example:

```
var cities = new List<string> { "Los Angeles",
  "Seattle", "New York", "San Francisco" };

var tasks = cities.ForEachAsync(async city =>
{
  return new { City = city, Weather = await
    GetWeatherForAsync(city) };
}, 2);
```

```
foreach (var task in tasks)
{
  var taskResult = await task;

  ProcessWeather(taskResult.City, taskResult.Weather);
}
```

These are the results:

```
[1:22:09 PM]: Getting the weather for 'Los Angeles'
[1:22:09 PM]: Getting the weather for 'Seattle'
```

Here the parallelism limit started to work. We will not run more tasks until one of them is completed:

```
[1:22:10 PM]: Processing weather for 'Los Angeles': 'Temp: 6C'
```

The first task has finished; now we can run one more task:

```
[1:22:10 PM]: Getting the weather for 'New York'
```

This task is completed at once:

```
[1:22:15 PM]: Processing weather for 'New York': 'Temp: 8C'
```

Here, we run one more task:

```
[1:22:15 PM]: Getting the weather for 'San Francisco'
```

Now the second task is completed:

```
[1:22:16 PM]: Processing weather for 'Seattle': 'Temp: 7C'
```

Here goes the last task:

```
[1:22:20 PM]: Processing weather for 'San Francisco': 'Temp: 4C'
```

This is the illustration of the previous process:

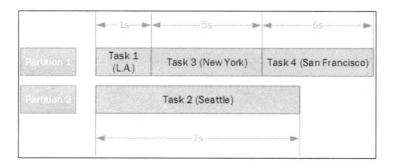

Here we have two partitions; each of these runs a set of tasks. The second partition is able to run only one task, because it runs for a long time. The first partition managed to run three tasks. The number of partitions limits the degree of parallelism.

Setting a task timeout

Operation cancellation support is built into the Task Parallel Library; many .NET Framework classes, as well as third-party code, support it and allow us to provide a cancellation mechanism in case an operation timeout happens. Some of these classes make programming easier and allow you to provide just a timeout value for the operation.

However, not all code has this potential. Besides this, we often operate with a task that has been already started and we cannot configure the timeout value in the operation. It is a very common problem and there is a solution for this:

```
public static async Task<T> WithTimeout<T>(this Task<T> task,
  TimeSpan timeout)
  {
  // Cover two corner cases: when task is completed and when
  // timeout is infinite
if (task.IsCompleted || timeout == Timeout.InfiniteTimeSpan)
{
    return await task;
  }

  var cts = new CancellationTokenSource();

  if (await Task.WhenAny(task, Task.Delay(timeout, cts.Token)) ==
    task)
  {
    cts.Cancel();
    return await task;
  }

  // Observe potential exception from the original task
  task.ContinueWith(_ => { },
    TaskContinuationOptions.ExecuteSynchronously);

  throw new TimeoutException();
  }
```

Now we can use the `WithTimeout` method on any task to set the timeout value for the operation. We can use this method like this:

```
try
{
  Weather weather = await
    WeatherService.GetWeatherAsync("New York").
    WithTimeout(TimeSpan.FromSeconds(2));

  ProcessWeather(weather);
}
catch (TimeoutException)
{
  Console.WriteLine("Task was timed out!");
}
```

The implementation looks simple, but there are a couple of important nuances:

- In the beginning, we check for situations where the task has been completed already, or we have an infinite timeout value. In this case, it is enough to use the C# **await** statement to get the task result in a safe manner.

- If the task completes before the timeout, we cancel the corresponding `Task.Delay` timer task. This looks like a slight optimization, but it can have a noticeable impact on the application performance.

- We try to observe the provided task exception, which is a very important thing to do. If we do not do so, we could easily cause `TaskScheduler.TaskUnobservedException` to be raised. In .NET 4.5+, it will not ruin your application at once, but it should be avoided anyway.

Asynchronous patterns

Since releasing the first version of C# and the .NET Framework, there has been built-in support for running asynchronous operations. Unfortunately, this infrastructure was quite complicated and hard to use, and this caused the next platform versions to include new ways (patterns) of writing asynchronous code that enhanced asynchronous programming experience.

Here, we will review three asynchronous programming patterns starting from the oldest:

- **APM**: Asynchronous Programming Model (introduced in the .NET Framework 1.0)
- **EAP**: Event-Based Asynchronous Pattern (released with the .NET Framework 2.0)
- **TAP**: Task-Based Asynchronous Pattern (appeared with the .NET Framework 4.0)

The first two patterns are usually considered as legacy code and should be used only in support scenarios where there is no possibility to use the task infrastructure from Task Parallel Library.

Asynchronous Programming Model

The **Asynchronous Programming Model (APM)** structure is as follows:

```
// Synchronous operation
public Result Operation(int input, ref int inOut, out int output);

// First method that denotes beginning of the asynchronous
//operation
public IAsyncResult BeginOperation(int input, ref int inOut, out int
output, AsyncCallback callback, object state);

// Second method that should be called when the operation is
//completed
public Result EndOperation(ref int inOut, out int output, IAsyncResult
asyncResult);
```

This pattern is structured in the following way: an asynchronous operation splits into two methods — BeginOperationName/EndOperationName, where the OperationName part is an actual name of this operation. The BeginOperationName method accepts input parameters, starts an asynchronous operation, and returns some kind of operation state that is represented by an object implementing IAsyncResult interface. Usually, it also accepts an additional operation context — the state parameter, and a callback that will be called when the operation completes.

To get the operation result and operation exception handling, we need to call the EndOperationName method. If the operation is already complete, this method will immediately return the result or throw an exception. If the operation is still running, this method call will be blocked until the operation completes.

IAsyncResult provides a WaitHandle instance that can be used to determine whether the operation has been completed, or whether the operation has completed synchronously.

As an example of using the APM pattern, let's implement the weather information service call and explain the code step by step:

```
public class WeatherService
{
  private readonly Func<string, Weather> _getWeatherFunc;
  public WeatherService()
  {
    _getWeatherFunc = GetWeather;
  }
  public Weather GetWeather(string city)
  {
    // Original synchronous implementation
  }

  public IAsyncResult BeginGetWeather(string city,
    AsyncCallback callback, object state) {
    return _getWeatherFunc.BeginInvoke(city, callback, state);
  }

  public Weather EndGetWeather(IAsyncResult asyncResult)
  {
    return _getWeatherFunc.EndInvoke(asyncResult);
  }
}
```

Here, in this example, we simulated an asynchronous operation with an asynchronous delegate invocation. The real APM implementation including remote service call details is too complicated, and it does not make sense to illustrate the APM pattern.

Then, we will write a client with APM:

```
var weatherServce = new WeatherService();

// Pseudo asynchronous call
string newYork = "New York";
IAsyncResult ar1 =
  weatherServce.BeginGetWeather(newYork, callback: null, state: null);

ar1.AsyncWaitHandle.WaitOne();
Weather weather1 = weatherServce.EndGetWeather(ar1);
```

```
ProcessWeather(newYork, weather1);

// Real asynchronous version
string seattle = "Seattle";
weatherServce.BeginGetWeather(seattle, callback: (IAsyncResult
  asyncResult) =>
  {
    var context = (Tuple<string,
      WeatherService>)asyncResult.AsyncState;

    try
    {
      Weather weather = context.Item2.EndGetWeather(asyncResult);
      ProcessWeather(context.Item1, weather);
    }
      catch (Exception e)
    {
      HandleWeatherError(e);
    }
  },
  state: Tuple.Create(seattle, weatherServce));
```

The first piece of code shows how we can call an asynchronous operation in the APM paradigm. We started with the `BeginGetWeather` method call, then immediately called `ar1.WaitHandle.WaitOne`. We can simply call `weatherService.EndGetWeather` instead and get the same result.

Then we used a real asynchronous operation call. We have used both the last input parameters of the `BeginGetWeather` method — `callback` and `state`. Notice that there is no context capture — the context gets into asynchronous operation through a `state` parameter.

The APM pattern has the following features:

- **Low-level pattern**: This was introduced in the first .NET Framework version and is used for many asynchronous operations in the Base Class Library.

- **Low performance overhead**: The callback method is called on the same thread where the asynchronous operation completed. No additional operations for synchronization context capturing occurs.

  Besides, it is very hard to combine several asynchronous operations, so one depends on another.

- **Coupling between the asynchronous operation provider and its consumers**: Asynchronous operation is not a first-class object. It is not possible to initiate the operation, then to pass it somehow to the other code and handle it there. A class that provides an asynchronous operation and its client classes have a tight connection. This, as well, makes unit testing for such operations very hard, since it is very hard to create a mock asynchronous operation.

The APM can be used in the following scenario—**only for legacy code support**. Task-based asynchronous patterns can do everything APM can do. Also they have a low performance overhead, but are modern and easy to use—especially with the C# **async/await** statements.

Event-based Asynchronous Pattern

An **Event-based Asynchronous Pattern (EAP)** structure is as follows:

```
// Synchronous operation
public Result Operation(int input, ref int inOut, out int output);

// Raised when the Operation finished (successfuly, with exception or
was cannelled)
public event EventHandler<OperationCompletedEventArgs>
OperationCompleted;

// Report execution progress
public event EventHandler<ProgressChangedEventArgs>
OperationProgressChanged;

// Method that starts asynchronous execution
public void OperationAsync(int input, ref int inOut);

// Method that starts asynchronous execution and gets additional user
defined state
public void OperationAsync(int input, ref int inOut, object
userState);

// Cancel pending operation
public void CancelAsync(object state);

public class OperationCompletedEventArgs: AsyncCompletedEventArgs
{
    public OperationCompletedEventArgs(
```

```
                    Exception error, bool cancelled, object userState)
                    : base(error, cancelled, userState)
            {
            }

        public Result Result { get; internal set; }
        public int InOut { get; internal set; }
        public int Output { get; internal set; }
    }
```

EAP was implemented in .NET Framework 2.0 and was designed to be used in application UI components. Most of the .NET types that implement this pattern inherit the `System.ComponentModel.Component` class as well and can be easily used with Windows Forms or WPF design-time editor.

The main idea behind EAP is to use events for notification about asynchronous operation completion. We start the operation with the `OperationNameAsync` method, and the completion event name is usually `OperationNameCompleted`. Besides this, there are other events, for example the `OperationProgressChanged` event that allows us to track the operation's execution progress.

An important feature of this pattern is that these events use the same synchronization context where the asynchronous operation has been started. If we use the UI thread to run this operation, then it is possible to use UI controls from the event handlers method of the component that implements EAP, which makes the code clean and comfortable to write.

Let's implement a weather information service with EAP:

```
public class WeatherService
{
    private bool _isOperationRunning = false;
    private readonly SendOrPostCallback _operationFinished;

    public WeatherService()
    {
        // This delegate should be called
        // in captured sync context
        _operationFinished = ProcessOperationFinished;
    }

    public Weather GetWeather(string city)
    {
        // Original synchronous implementation
    }
```

```csharp
public event EventHandler<GetWeatherCompletedEventArgs>
  GetWeatherCompleted;

public void GetWeatherAsync(string city, object userState)
{
  if (_isOperationRunning)
    throw new InvalidOperationException();

 _isOperationRunning = true;
 AsyncOperation operation = AsyncOperationManager
  .CreateOperation(userState);

  // Running GetWeather asynchronously
  ThreadPool.QueueUserWorkItem(state =>
  {
    GetWeatherCompletedEventArgs args = null;
    try
    {
      var weather = GetWeather(city);
      args = new GetWeatherCompletedEventArgs(weather, state);
    }
    catch (Exception e)
    {
        args = new GetWeatherCompletedEventArgs(e, state);
      }

      // Using AsyncOperation that will marshal control
      // flow to the synchronization context that was
      // captured at the beginning of this method.

      operation.PostOperationCompleted(_operationFinished,
        args);

  }, userState);
}

private void ProcessOperationFinished(object state)
{
  // Mark that current operation is completed
  _isOperationRunning = false;

  var args = (GetWeatherCompletedEventArgs)state;
```

```
        var handler = GetWeatherCompleted;
          if (handler != null)
            handler(this, args);
    }
  }
```

The GetWeatherAsync method contains the main pattern logic. First, we created the AsyncOperation object, where we captured the current synchronization context with SynchronizationContext.Current. Then, we used the ThreadPool. QueueUserWorkItem method to run the GetWeather operation asynchronously on a thread pool. Then we used operation.PostOperationCompleted to post a notification about operation completion on the captured synchronization context. This will allow event subscribers to handle the GetWeatherCompleted event safely and will make it possible to use UI controls without using the Control.Invoke and Dispatcher.BeginInvoke mechanics.

Now let's look at how to use the service with EAP:

```
var weatherService = new WeatherService();
var city = "New York";

// Start asynchronous operation
weatherService.GetWeatherAsync(city, userState: null);

// If current method is running in UI thread
// following event handler would be executed in the UI thread
weatherService.GetWeatherCompleted += (sender, args) => {
  Weather result = args.Result;
  ProcessWeather(city, result);
};
```

The EAP features are as follows:

- **High-level pattern**: EAP allows us to consume asynchronous operations with ease as well as start new ones
- **High overhead**: Since operation completion events always get posted to the captured synchronization context, this pattern is not intended to be used from low-level components that do intensive IO operations
- **Intended for UI components**: Since EAP was designed for a very specific scenario (UI components), it might not be the best choice to program some other features

- **Complicated implementation**: While this is definitely easier than APM, it is still hard to program real-world scenarios with operation progress and cancellation

- **Coupling between asynchronous operation provider and its consumers**: Similar to the previous pattern, this one also creates tight coupling between the operation class and client classes

EAP can used in the following scenario—**legacy code support**. Nevertheless, if you write a new code you should not use EAP. Task-based async pattern has everything that EAP has, but it also has language level support, loose coupling, and a lot of other useful features.

Task-based Asynchronous Pattern

Task Parallel Library has been existing since the .NET Framework 4.0 release, and it introduced a new asynchronous programming pattern—**Task-based Asynchronous Pattern (TAP)**. This pattern consists of the following methods:

```
// Synchronous operation
public Result Operation(int input, ref int inOut, out int output);

// Asynchronous version
public Task<WrappedResult> OperationAsync(int input, int inOut);

// Custom result that wraps in/out and out parameters
public class WrappedResult
{
  public Result Result { get; internal set; }
  public int InOut { get; internal set; }
  public int Output { get; internal set; }
}
```

Similar to EAP, TAP uses the same naming scheme. Operations are named `OperationNameAsync` by adding the `Async` suffix to the synchronous implementation name. However, the main idea behind TAP is to use a special `Task` object that represents an asynchronous operation without any return value, and `Task<T>` for those that return results of the `T` type. Since we can access the result only through the Task.Result property, every input and output parameter must be a part of the return value.

The following is one more weather information service implementation:

```
public class WeatherService
{
  public Weather GetWeather(string city)
  {
    // Original synchronous implementation
  }
  public Task<Weather> GetWeatherAsync(string city)
  {
    return Task.Run(() => GetWeather(city));
  }
}
```

The easiest implementation that seems to be obvious is to wrap a synchronous method into a task with the help of the `Task.Run` method. However, this approach should not be used in real-world applications, unless you are completely sure about what is going on.

 This antipattern is called "async over sync" and using this will lead to scalability and performance problems in your application. Most of the truly asynchronous operations in the .NET Framework are IO-bound, and thus do not require using additional threads. This topic will be reviewed in detail in *Chapter 8, Server-Side Asynchrony*.

Let's look at the following code:

```
public async Task ProcessWeatherFromWeatherService()
{
  var weatherService = new WeatherService();
  string city = "San Francisco";

  // If this method was called in the UI thread,
  // "awaiter" will capture synchronization context
  // and ProcessWeather method would be called in the UI thread as
  // well

  Weather weather = await weatherService.GetWeatherAsync(city);
  ProcessWeather(city, weather);
}
```

Task-based Asynchronous Pattern is now the most popular and most convenient way to develop asynchronous applications. It can be characterized by the following:

- **Low overhead**: Tasks have low overhead and can be used in high-load scenarios.

- **High-level**: Task is a high level abstraction that provides a convenient API to combine asynchronous operations, to capture or not capture the current synchronization context if needed, convert older APM and EAP patterns to TAP, and many other features.

- **Comfortable to use**: This pattern is easy to use by developers, but at the same time, it has a rich API and more features than the previous two.

- **Language support in C#/VB**: C# and VB.NET has built-in **async/await** statements that make asynchronous programming much easier. This infrastructure is based on the Task and Task<T> types.

> As we saw in *Chapter 5, C# Language Support for Asynchrony*, **await** can be used with any type that has its own method or an extension method called GetAwaiter without parameters, which returns the object that implements the INotifyCompletion interface and contains the IsCompleted Boolean property and the GetResult method with no parameters.

- **Task and Task<T> are first-class objects**: Unlike previous patterns, a task instance is self-sufficient. It can be passed as a parameter to other methods or can be stored in a variable or instance field. If you have access to the task instance, you will have full control over the corresponding asynchronous operation. We do not need to use the asynchronous operation class a second time to finish the operation. We can test such operations and return an already completed task from a mock method.

- **Getting rid of side effects**: Using the Task<T> class encourages the avoidance of side effects in the program, which is very important to reduce contention and improve scalability.

Concurrent patterns

We have already reviewed some of these patterns earlier in this book. For example, in *Chapter 4, Task Parallel Library in Depth*, we studied Parallel.Invoke and Parallel.Foreach, which actually is an implementation of the **fork/join** pattern. In *Chapter 6, Using Concurrent Data Structures*, we reviewed a **Producer/Consumer** pattern implementation. However, there is a very important scenario that we have not seen yet. It is called a **parallel pipeline**.

Parallel pipelines

Usually a complex parallel computation can be considered as several stages combined into some sort of a pipeline. The latter stage needs the results of the former, and this prevents these stages from running in parallel. However, the calculations inside each stage can be independent, which allows us to parallelize each stage itself. Besides this, we can simultaneously run all the stages, assuming that we can process stage results one by one, so we do not have to wait until each stage computes all the results before proceeding to the next stage. Instead of this, we get an item from a previous stage as soon as it is ready and pass it along to the next stage, and so on and so forth, until the final stage. This way of organizing parallel computations is known as **parallel pipeline**, which is a special case of a Producer/Consumer pattern. It allows us to achieve almost parallel processing of stage computations, shifted by the time that is required to get the first stage result.

The following code shows how to implement a **parallel pipeline** using a standard BlockingCollection data structure:

```
private const int ParallelismDegree = 4;
private const int Count = 1;

static void Main(string[] args){
  var cts = new CancellationTokenSource();

  Task.Run(() => {
    if (Console.ReadKey().KeyChar == 'c') {
      cts.Cancel();
    }
  });

  var sourceArrays = new BlockingCollection<string>[
    ParallelismDegree];
  for (int i = 0; i < sourceArrays.Length; i++) {
    sourceArrays[i] = new BlockingCollection<string>(Count);
  }

  var getWeatherStep = new PipelineWorkerAsync<string, Weather> (
    sourceArrays,
    city => WeatherService.GetWeatherAsync(city),
    cts.Token,
    "Get Weather",
    Count
  );
```

```
var convertTempStep = new PipelineWorkerAsync<Weather,
  Tuple<string, decimal>> (
  getWeatherStep.Output,
  weather => Task.FromResult(Tuple.Create(weather.City,
    weather.TemperatureCelcius * (decimal)9/5 + 32)),
  cts.Token,
  "Convert Temperature",
  Count
);

var printInfoStep = new PipelineWorkerAsync<Tuple<string,
  decimal>, string> (
  convertTempStep.Output,
  t => Console.WriteLine("The temperature in {0} is {1}F on
    thread id {2}", t.Item1, t.Item2,
      Thread.CurrentThread.ManagedThreadId),
      cts.Token,
      "Print Information"
  );

try {
  Parallel.Invoke(
    () => {
      Parallel.ForEach(
        new[] {"Seattle", "New York", "Los Angeles",
          "San Francisco"},
          (city, state) => {
            if (cts.Token.IsCancellationRequested) {
              state.Stop();
            }

            AddCityToSourceCollection(sourceArrays, city,
              cts.Token);
          });
          foreach (var arr in sourceArrays) {
            arr.CompleteAdding();
          }
      },
      () => getWeatherStep.RunAsync().GetAwaiter().GetResult(),
      () => convertTempStep.RunAsync().GetAwaiter().GetResult(),
      () => printInfoStep.RunAsync().GetAwaiter().GetResult()
    );
}
catch (AggregateException ae) {
```

```
        foreach (var ex in ae.InnerExceptions)
          Console.WriteLine(ex.Message + ex.StackTrace);
      }

      if (cts.Token.IsCancellationRequested) {
        Console.WriteLine("Operation has been canceled! Press ENTER to
          exit.");
      }
      else {
        Console.WriteLine("Press ENTER to exit.");
      }
      Console.ReadLine();
    }

    static void AddCityToSourceCollection
      BlockingCollection<string>[] cities, string city,
      CancellationToken token) {
        BlockingCollection<string>.TryAddToAny(cities, city, 50,
          token);
      Console.WriteLine("Added {0} to fetch weather on thread id
        {1}", city, Thread.CurrentThread.ManagedThreadId);

      Thread.Sleep(TimeSpan.FromMilliseconds(100));
    }
```

At the beginning of the preceding code, we are implementing a cancellation operation for the pipeline by running a separate task that is listening for the *C* key press. When the user presses the *C* button, the task runs `cts.Cancel` that signals a cancellation operation to the shared cancellation token. This token goes into all the further operations and is able to cancel the entire parallel pipeline at once.

Now, we define the pipeline behavior. First, we set the parallelism degree for our parallel pipeline. In the following example, we will create four blocking collections for one element each. It will cause four elements to be processed in parallel. If we need to change this, we can use two collections for two elements, and so on.

Next, we will define pipeline steps. The first step is responsible for getting weather information for each city that appears in the source collection. Then the next step will convert the temperature from Celsius to Fahrenheit. The final step will print out the weather information to the console.

All we need to do now is run the entire pipeline. We will use the `Parallel.Invoke` statement to run all the pipeline stages in parallel, and in the first stage, we will use `Parallel.Foreach` to fill in the `cities` collection in parallel as well:

```
class PipelineWorkerAsync<TInput, TOutput>
{
  Func<TInput, Task<TOutput>> _processorAsync = null;
  Action<TInput> _outputProcessor = null;
  BlockingCollection<TInput>[] _input;
  CancellationToken _token;
  private int _count;

  public PipelineWorkerAsync(
    BlockingCollection<TInput>[] input,
    Func<TInput, Task<TOutput>> processorAsync,
    CancellationToken token,
    string name,
    int count)
    {
      _input = input;
      _count = count;
      _processorAsync = processorAsync;
      _token = token;

      Output = new BlockingCollection<TOutput>[_input.Length];
      for (int i = 0; i < Output.Length; i++)
        Output[i] = null == input[i] ? null: new
          BlockingCollection <TOutput>(Count);

      Name = name;
    }

  public PipelineWorkerAsync(
    BlockingCollection<TInput>[] input,
    Action<TInput> renderer,
    CancellationToken token,
    string name) {
      _input = input;
      _outputProcessor = renderer;
      _token = token;
      Name = name;
      Output = null;
    }
```

```
public BlockingCollection<TOutput>[]
   Output { get; private set; }

public string Name { get; private set; }

public async Task RunAsync() {
  Console.WriteLine("{0} is running", this.Name);
  List<Task> tasks = new List<Task>();
  foreach (var bc in _input) {
    var local = bc;
    var t = Task.Run(new Func<Task>(async () => {
      TInput receivedItem;
      while (!local.IsCompleted &&
        !_token.IsCancellationRequested) {
        var ok = local.TryTake(out receivedItem, 50, _token);

        if (ok) {
          if (Output != null) {
            TOutput outputItem = await _processorAsync(
              receivedItem);
            BlockingCollection<TOutput>.AddToAny(Output,
              outputItem);

            Console.WriteLine("{0} sent {1} to next, on thread
            id {2}",Name, outputItem,
            Thread.CurrentThread.ManagedThreadId);

            Thread.Sleep(TimeSpan.FromMilliseconds(100));
          }
          else {
            _outputProcessor(receivedItem);
          }
        }
        else {
          Thread.Sleep(TimeSpan.FromMilliseconds(50));
        }
      }
    }),
    _token);

    tasks.Add(t);
  }

  await Task.WhenAll(tasks);
```

```
      if (Output != null) {
        foreach (var bc in Output) bc.CompleteAdding();
      }
    }
  }
}
```

The pipeline step logic is defined inside the `PipelineWorkerAsync` class. We have created the worker instance, providing it with the input collections and a transformation function that gets an initial value and calculates the result. Then we ran collection processing in parallel. While we processed each collection, we passed calculation results to the output collections of the next step in our pipeline. This happens until the final step has been reached, which just prints results to the console.

Summary

In this chapter, we have considered the different kinds of asynchronous programming patterns—from the smallest ones such as a task with timeout to the large multipurpose parallel pipeline pattern. We have reviewed the history of asynchronous programming in the .NET Framework and C#, and went step by step through all existing patterns including APM, EAP, and TAP.

In the next chapter, we will cover a very important topic of server-side asynchronous programming. We will learn about scalability, performance metrics, details of IO-bound and CPU-bound asynchronous operations, and how the slightest mistake can ruin your backend. Also, we will learn a couple of tricks that will allow us to detect possible scalability problems and avoid them.

8
Server-side Asynchrony

In this chapter, we will show how a server application is different from other applications, what scalability is, and how it is important. We will look at the .NET HTTP API server application framework, learn to use Visual Studio to create load tests, dig into asynchronous I/O details, and review important nuances such as synchronization context. Finally, we will suggest an architectural pattern for a server application to run long operations and remain scalable and performant.

Server applications

A **server application** can be defined as an application that accepts requests, processes them, and sends the corresponding responses to the client. Communication happens via some transport protocols, and usually, but not necessarily, the client and server applications are situated on different physical computers. The computer that runs the server application is usually referred to as the server.

There are many types of server applications. For example, a Remote Desktop Services software that allows us to open remote session to a Windows machine is a server application. Each user connection consumes a lot of server resources, but in this particular scenario, this is inevitable. This server application does not need to support hundreds or thousands of simultaneous users and is intended to be like this. However, if we imagine a website that allows only a few users to browse it simultaneously, it would be definitely a failure.

On the other hand, it is OK when a website user gets notifications from the server with a delay of 2-3 seconds, but if we try to work with a remote desktop connection that shows updates from the server with such a delay, it would be very uncomfortable. There are different metrics that characterize a server application, and in different scenarios different metrics are important. One of the most important server application characteristics is **scalability**. Here is how this term is defined in Wikipedia:

Scalability is the ability of a system, network, or process to handle a growing amount of work in a capable manner or its ability to be enlarged to accommodate that growth.

Imagine that we have a website and it handles a certain number of concurrent users. To handle more users, we can try to add more memory and maybe install a new CPU with more cores to the server. If this allows us to achieve this goal, we can say that the application is able to **scale vertically**. If we can install more servers and make our application run on multiple machines and handle more users, this kind of scalability is called **horizontal scalability**. The following diagram shows the vertical and horizontal scalability:

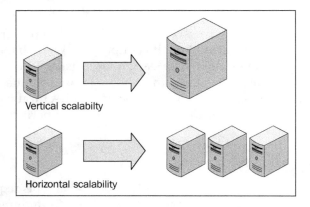

It may seem that every server application should scale in both ways, but usually this is not what happens. This topic is very interesting and vast, and it is worth writing another book on this. Let's state that most general-purpose server applications nowadays are web applications and services, so later we will review the ASP.NET web platform and specifically the OWIN Web API framework.

The OWIN Web API framework

In this chapter, we will concentrate on the ASP.NET platform. At the time of writing this book, ASP.NET 5 was not released. However, the OWIN project existed, and the code looked almost the same as in ASP.NET 5. So this was used to write the sample server applications. When ASP.NET 5 will be released, it will be easy to convert this code to the new platform. We will not go into the details of **OWIN**; it is an acronym for **Open Web Interface for .NET**, and basically, it is a way to compose application components with each other. It is a part of the ASP.NET ecosystem, and all we need to know for now is that with OWIN we can write HTTP services.

When we use ASP.NET, we see a typical HTTP application platform. First, there is an HTTP host that accepts incoming connections from clients. It can be a full Internet Information Services web server, or it can be a simple HTTP listener hosted in a usual .NET process. After the incoming HTTP request is processed by the HTTP host, it goes to the ASP.NET infrastructure. It gets a worker thread from the .NET thread pool and starts request data processing on this thread.

First, it tries to define what code will be handling this request by matching the request URL to existing routes. A route describes how URL parts correlate to web application code parts. A logical set of server code is called a controller. In the OWIN Web API framework, a controller contains a number of actions — methods that handle different HTTP requests usually by HTTP verbs (or by other rules that can be set in routes). Before all this becomes too complicated, let's look at the code. In the samples directory, it is located in the **Chapter 8** solution folder in the **AsyncServer** project. To leverage OWIN, we need to install the `Microsoft.AspNet.WebApi.OwinSelfHost` NuGet package. The first part is the entry code for the entire OWIN application:

```
public class Startup
{
  public void Configuration(IAppBuilder appBuilder)
  {
    var config = new HttpConfiguration();
    config.Routes.MapHttpRoute(
      "DefaultApi",
      "api/{controller}/{id}",
      new {id = RouteParameter.Optional});

    appBuilder.UseWebApi(config);
  }
}
```

Here we have configured our OWIN application by providing a default route. It will match URLs such as `http://hostname/api/somename/5` to a class called `SomenameController` that contains the `Get` method (if the request verb was HTTP GET) and will call this method providing a parameter `id` = `5` into it. The last line instructs OWIN to use a Web API component in the application.

Now let's look at the controller:

```
public class BadAsyncController : ApiController
{
  private readonly AsyncLib _client;

  public BadAsyncController()
  {
    _client = new AsyncLib();
  }

  public async Task<HttpResponseMessage> Get()
  {
    var sw = Stopwatch.StartNew();
    string value = await _client.BadMethodAsync();
    sw.Stop();
    var timespan = sw.Elapsed;
    return Request.CreateResponse(HttpStatusCode.OK,
      new
      {
      Message = value,
      Time = timespan
    });
  }
}
```

Here, we see the `Get` method code, which calls a library's asynchronous method and measures the time it took to complete. Then it returns an anonymous object containing the response data. It will be serialized to the JSON format by default.

We will define another controller, which will be different only with respect to an asynchronous library's method name that it calls:

```
public class GoodAsyncController : ApiController
{
  private readonly AsyncLib _client;

  public GoodAsyncController()
  {
    _client = new AsyncLib();
```

```
    }

    public async Task<HttpResponseMessage> Get()
    {
      var sw = Stopwatch.StartNew();
      string value = await _client.GoodMethodAsync();
      sw.Stop();
      var timespan = sw.Elapsed;
      return Request.CreateResponse(HttpStatusCode.OK,
      new
      {
        Message = value,
        Time = timespan
      });
    }
  }
}
```

Here we have called `GoodMethodAsync`. We will describe both controllers later, but now we need to run the application. We need to create an application host:

```
class Program
{
  static void Main(string[] args)
  {
    string baseAddress = "http://localhost:9000/";

    using (WebApp.Start<Startup>(url: baseAddress))
    {
      HttpClient client = new HttpClient();

      var response = client.GetAsync(baseAddress +
        "api/GoodAsync").Result;

      Console.WriteLine(response);
      Console.WriteLine(
        response.Content.ReadAsStringAsync().Result);
      Console.WriteLine();

      response = client.GetAsync(baseAddress +
        "api/BadAsync").Result;

      Console.WriteLine(response);
      Console.WriteLine(
        response.Content.ReadAsStringAsync().Result);
```

```
            Console.ReadLine();
        }
    }
}
```

This code starts a web application on a localhost on port 9000. If this port is already taken, there will be an exception. In this case, just change the port number. After the application starts, we will issue two HTTP requests and see the results on the console window. Both requests should complete without any issues and show that it took two seconds for them to complete. You can use a regular web browser to open `http://localhost:9000` and see the results. Internet Explorer is not very good with JSON, but Google Chrome will show you a JSON result with good formatting. Besides this, there is a very useful Google Chrome extension called Postman. This can issue different HTTP requests and is very comfortable to use; it is shown in the following screenshot:

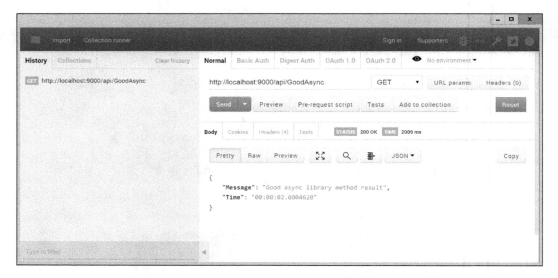

Load testing and scalability

We see that both the controllers have behaved the same so far. However, what about scalability? To check how well the application scales, we need to have many requests from many users. We will be able to do this with the help of different tools. First, we can use Visual Studio, but it requires the Ultimate edition (or the Enterprise edition for Visual Studio 2015) where web test tools are available. If you have it, then you can create a new project and choose the **Web Performance and Load Test** project from the test category. In the samples folder, there is an already created test project that is called **AsyncServerTests**. Now we need to create Web Performance Test. After creating, it will run in the browser and try to record your test. You can record it from the browser or stop the recording and add a new request as shown in the following screenshot; then in **Properties** provide a full URL to see what have we tested so far:

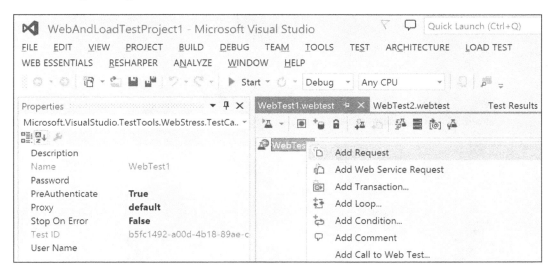

Next, we need to create a load test. When we add a new load test, it will show a wizard with different options. We need to choose a constant load pattern and set the number of users to 1000. Then, in the test mix, we have to pick a web test that we have just created. Finally, in the run settings set the warm-up duration to 15 seconds, and set duration time to 2 minutes. Click on **Finish** and repeat all this for another controller. When everything is set, let's run a load test for GoodAsyncController. The output is as shown in the following screenshot:

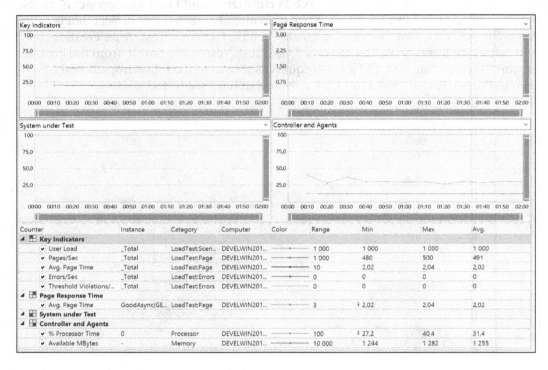

These data show that for 1000 users per second, the average response time was still about two seconds. This is a very good result and shows that GoodAsyncController scales well and is able to handle many concurrent requests. To compare this to BadAsyncController, we need to create a web and load test for this, and then run the load test.

Before doing so, if we do not have the Visual Studio Ultimate edition, it is still possible to load test our web application. The easiest way is to use the Apache bench command line tool. It is included in the Apache web server installation, but if you do not need it, you can download **xampp** (a preconfigured Apache distributive) that has a portable installation option. This means that you can download a zip archive from the xampp site, and then extract it to somewhere in your file system. You will find the `ab.exe` tool in the `xampp\apache\bin` folder. It has many parameters, but we can use just two of them — the number of concurrent requests and the time for the benchmark. Here we have issued 1,000 concurrent requests for 2 minutes to our `GoodAsyncController`:

```
ab -c 1000 -t 120 http://localhost:9000/api/GoodAsync
```

The output shown will be the same — the average request time will be around 2 seconds.

Now let's see the performance test results for `BadAsyncController`. The following screenshot shows the performance test results:

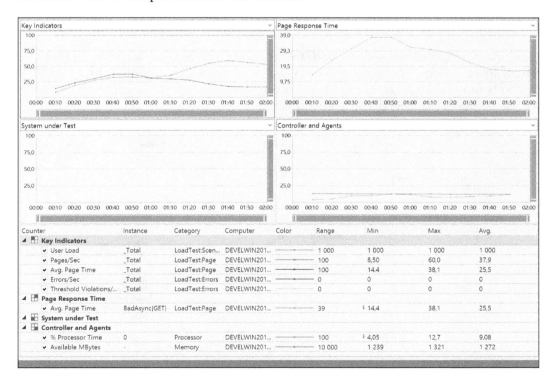

Here the picture is different. We see that the average request time is more than ten times higher than in the previous test. Obviously, this code does not scale as well as `GoodAsyncController` does. Since the codes inside the controllers are identical, and the only difference is the asynchronous library method that was called, it makes sense to look into this library and see what is going on:

```
public class AsyncLib
{
  public async Task<string> GoodMethodAsync()
  {
    await Task.Delay(TimeSpan.FromSeconds(2));
    return "Good async library method result";
  }

  public async Task<string> BadMethodAsync()
  {
    Thread.Sleep(TimeSpan.FromSeconds(2));
    return "Bad async library method result";
  }
}
```

The code is actually very simple. Both the methods wait for two seconds, and then return string results. However, we can see that `Thread.Sleep` is obviously the reason behind bad scalability. In the diagram, you can see what is going on when we use `BadMethodAsync` in our web application:

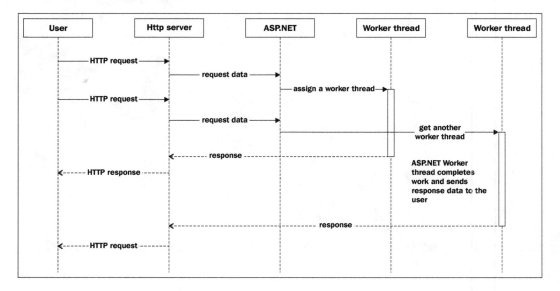

Each worker thread starts running our code and waits two seconds doing nothing. Then, they return the response. As we may recall from the previous chapters, thread pool worker threads are a limited resource, and when we start issuing 1,000 concurrent requests in a short time, all the worker threads become occupied running `Thread.Sleep`. At the same time, `GoodAsyncController` behaves differently. This can be seen in the following diagram:

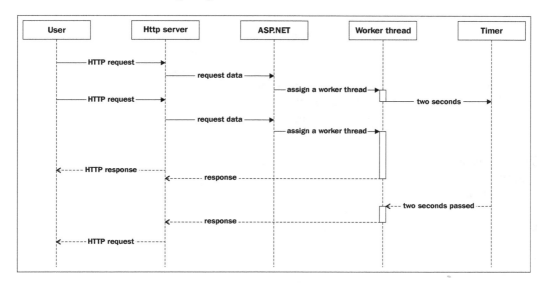

`Task.Delay` uses a timer object under the hood. This allows an ASP.NET worker thread to start a wait operation, and then to return to the application pool and process some other requests. When two seconds pass, the timer posts a continuation callback to an available ASP.NET thread pool worker thread. This allows the application to process more user requests, since worker threads are not blocked. So, this timer object helps our application to remain fast and scalable.

I/O and CPU-bound tasks

If we consider any CPU-intensive work that our server application can run instead of `Thread.Sleep`, we will find that this application will suffer from the same problem. Worker threads will become busy quite quickly, and there is not much that we can do about this. We can try to change our application logic to work around this problem, and we will get back to this problem at the end of the chapter.

However, besides CPU-bound operations, there are tasks related to input/ output processes, such as reading or writing a file, issuing a network request, or even performing a query against a database. These operations usually take much more time compared to CPU-bound work, and potentially they should be more problematic to our server application. I/O-bound work can take seconds. So does this mean that our worker threads will be locked for a longer time and the application will fail to scale?

Fortunately, there is one more component of the I/O-bound operation. When we mention a file or network request, we know that there are physical devices such as disks and network cards that actually execute these operations. These devices have controllers, and a controller in this context means a micro-computer with its own CPU. To perform an I/O-bound task, we do not need to waste the main CPU's time, it is enough to give all the required data to the I/O device controller, and it will perform the I/O operation and return the results with the help of a device driver.

To communicate with the I/O devices, Windows uses a special object called **I/O Completion Port** (or **IOCP**). It behaves pretty much like a timer, but the signals are coming from the I/O devices and not from the internal clock. This means that, while an I/O operation is in progress, we can reuse the ASP.NET worker thread to serve other requests, and thus achieve good scalability. The following diagram depicts the processes graphically:

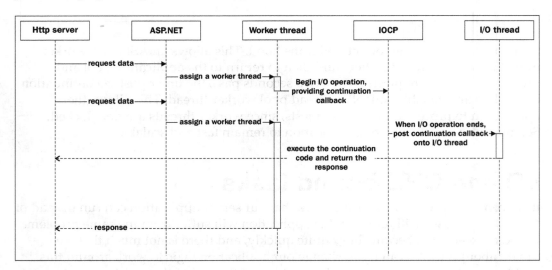

Notice a new entity called the I/O thread in the preceding diagram. There is a separate smaller pool of I/O threads inside this .NET thread pool. The I/O threads are not different from the usual worker threads, but they are being used only to execute continuation callbacks for asynchronous I/O operations. If we use general worker threads for this purpose, it can happen that there are no worker threads available and we cannot complete the I/O operation, which in turn will lead to deadlocks. Using a separate thread pool will help to prevent this, but we also need to be very careful not to cause I/O threads starvation. Look at the following example.

Here we will create an HTTP GET request for the Google site. As we have already learned, when we use `await`, all the code following the line with `await` gets wrapped in a continuation callback and is called when the asynchronous operation completes. Here we will use `Thread.Sleep` to see which threads will get busy:

```
private static async Task<string> IssueHttpRequest()
{
  var str = await new HttpClient().GetStringAsync(
    "http://google.com");
  Thread.Sleep(5000);
  return str;
}
```

Then, we need to get information about what is happening with thread pool threads. Fortunately, a .NET thread pool has a set of static methods that allow us to get some information about worker and I/O threads in a thread pool:

```
private static void PrintThreadCounts()
{
  int ioThreads;
  int maxIoThreads;
  int workerThreads;
  int maxWorkerThreads;

  ThreadPool.GetMaxThreads(out maxWorkerThreads, out
    maxIoThreads);
  ThreadPool.GetAvailableThreads(out workerThreads, out
    ioThreads);

  Console.WriteLine(
    "Worker threads: {0}, I/O threads: {1}, Total threads: {2}",
    maxWorkerThreads - workerThreads,
    maxIoThreads - ioThreads,
    Process.GetCurrentProcess().Threads.Count
  );
}
```

In the `Main` method, we will run many asynchronous I/O tasks; while iterating through all these tasks to complete in each second, we will print out information about thread pool threads:

```
private static void Main(string[] args)
{
  var tasks = new List<Task<string>>();

  for (var i = 0; i < 100; i++)
  {
    tasks.Add(Task.Run(() =>
    {
      // Thread.Sleep(5000);
      return IssueHttpRequest();
    }));
  }

  var allComplete = Task.WhenAll(tasks);

  while (allComplete.Status != TaskStatus.RanToCompletion)
  {
    Thread.Sleep(1000);
    PrintThreadCounts();
  }

  Console.WriteLine(tasks[0].Result.Substring(0, 160));
}
```

If we run this code (among the other samples for **Chapter 8**; this one is called **IOThreadsTest**), it will show that the I/O thread number will slowly increase until some point and go back to zero. To prove that the I/O operation really happens, the last lines will be the beginning of the Google web page HTML content. If we now comment out the first `Thread.Sleep` call and uncomment it in the `Main` method, the situation will be different. We will block worker threads, and the I/O thread number will remain low.

Deep dive into asynchronous I/O

Usually, there is no need to use Win32 API to start an asynchronous I/O operation. The .NET base class library has many APIs that are comfortable to use, and leverage asynchronous I/O. The following code is not intended to be used in a production software, it just shows how such an API can be written in case you do not have it in the .NET Framework.

First, we need to allow an unsafe code in our project. The setting is inside the project properties of the **Build** section as shown in the following screenshot:

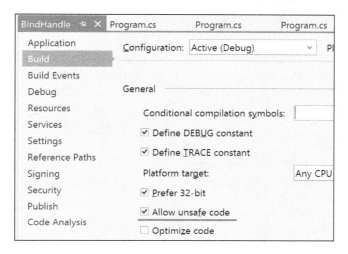

Here, we need to define many data structures for the API function calls. The fully working code can be found in the **BindHandle** sample project. In this book, we will skip the unimportant details.

First, we need to use P/Invoke for two Windows API functions:

```
[DllImport("kernel32.dll", SetLastError = true, CharSet =
  CharSet.Auto)]
public static extern SafeFileHandle CreateFile(
    string lpFileName,
    EFileAccess dwDesiredAccess,
    EFileShare dwShareMode,
    IntPtr lpSecurityAttributes,
    ECreationDisposition dwCreationDisposition,
    EFileAttributes dwFlagsAndAttributes,
    SafeFileHandle hTemplateFile);

[DllImport("kernel32.dll", SetLastError = true)]
unsafe internal static extern int ReadFile(
  SafeFileHandle handle,
  byte* bytes,
  int numBytesToRead,
  IntPtr numBytesRead_mustBeZero,
  NativeOverlapped* overlapped);
```

Then, we create a file and write some text in it in the usual way:

```
using (var sw = File.CreateText("test.txt"))
{
   sw.WriteLine("Test!");
}
```

Here, we are opening this file for asynchronous reading. Notice `EFileAttributes`. `Overlapped` in the method parameters. If we want an asynchronous I/O operation, we must specify this flag:

```
SafeFileHandle handle = CreateFile(
   "test.txt",
   EFileAccess.FILE_GENERIC_READ,
   EFileShare.Read | EFileShare.Write | EFileShare.Delete,
   (IntPtr)null,
   ECreationDisposition.OpenExisting,
   EFileAttributes.Overlapped,
   new SafeFileHandle(IntPtr.Zero, false));
```

Now we bind the file handle to a .NET thread pool. It maintains an I/O completion port, and this handle will be attached to the port:

```
if (!ThreadPool.BindHandle(handle))
{
   Console.WriteLine("Failed to bind handle to the threadpool.");
   return;
}
```

We need to prepare a buffer for the file that is going to be read. The following code checks whether the buffer is empty:

```
byte[] bytes = new byte[0x8000];

Console.WriteLine("First byte in buffer: {0}", bytes[0]);
```

Now, we need to prepare a callback that will be executed after the asynchronous operation completes. If everything is fine, we will get file content from the buffer and print it to the console. We must clean up the resources after the operation completion:

```
IOCompletionCallback iocomplete = delegate(uint errorCode, uint
   numBytes, NativeOverlapped* nativeOverlapped)
   {
      try
      {
         if (errorCode != 0 && numBytes != 0)
```

```
    {
      Console.WriteLine("Error {0} when reading file.",
        errorCode);
    }
    Console.WriteLine("Read {0} bytes.", numBytes);
    Console.WriteLine(
      Encoding.UTF8.GetChars(
        new ArraySegment<byte>(bytes,0,
          (int)numBytes).ToArray()));
  }
  finally
  {
    Overlapped.Unpack(nativeOverlapped);
    Overlapped.Free(nativeOverlapped);
  }
};
```

Here, we have prepared a data structure to be passed to the asynchronous operation start. We have to pin our buffer's address to memory, so the pointer will be valid:

```
Overlapped overlapped = new Overlapped();

NativeOverlapped* pOverlapped = overlapped.Pack(iocomplete,
  bytes);

pOverlapped->OffsetLow = 0;

fixed (byte* p = bytes)
{
  // Here we start asynchronously reading the file.
  // When the operation will complete, ioComplete
  // callback will be called
  int r = ReadFile(handle, p, bytes.Length, IntPtr.Zero,
    pOverlapped);

  if (r == 0)
  {
    r = Marshal.GetLastWin32Error();
    if (r != ERROR_IO_PENDING)
    {
      Console.WriteLine("Failed to read file. LastError is {0}",
        Marshal.GetLastWin32Error());
      Overlapped.Unpack(pOverlapped);
      Overlapped.Free(pOverlapped);
      return;
```

```
        }
      }
    }
```

When we run this code, we will see that the file content has been successfully read.

Real and fake asynchronous I/O operations

So far, an asynchronous I/O seems to be a good thing for server applications. Unfortunately, there is quite unexpected underwater stone that is very hard to find. Let's look at the following code. It happens that the `FileStream` instance has the `IsAsync` property, indicating that the underlying I/O operation is asynchronous. We will start a few asynchronous writes and check whether they are really asynchronous:

```
private const int BUFFER_SIZE = 4096;

private static async Task ProcessAsynchronousIO()
{
  using (var stream = new FileStream("test1.txt", FileMode.Create,
    FileAccess.ReadWrite, FileShare.None, BUFFER_SIZE))
  {
    Console.WriteLine("1. Uses I/O Threads: {0}", stream.IsAsync);

    var buffer = Encoding.UTF8.GetBytes(CreateFileContent());
    var t = stream.WriteAsync(buffer, 0, buffer.Length);
    await t;
  }

  using (var stream = new FileStream("test2.txt", FileMode.Create,
    FileAccess.ReadWrite, FileShare.None, BUFFER_SIZE,
      FileOptions.Asynchronous))
  {
    Console.WriteLine("2. Uses I/O Threads: {0}", stream.IsAsync);

    var buffer = Encoding.UTF8.GetBytes(CreateFileContent());
    var t = stream.WriteAsync(buffer, 0, buffer.Length);
    await t;
  }

  using (var stream = File.Create("test3.txt", BUFFER_SIZE,
    FileOptions.Asynchronous))
```

```
using (var sw = new StreamWriter(stream))
{
    Console.WriteLine("3. Uses I/O Threads: {0}", stream.IsAsync);

    await sw.WriteAsync(CreateFileContent());
}

using (var sw = new StreamWriter("test4.txt", append: true))
{
    Console.WriteLine("4. Uses I/O Threads: {0}", ((FileStream)
        sw.BaseStream).IsAsync);

    await sw.WriteAsync(CreateFileContent());
}

Console.WriteLine("Deleting files...");

var deleteTasks = new Task[4];
for (var i = 0; i < 4; i++)
{
    var fileName = string.Format("test{0}.txt", i + 1);
    deleteTasks[i] = SimulateAsynchronousDelete(fileName);
}

await Task.WhenAll(deleteTasks);

Console.WriteLine("Deleting complete.");
}

private static string CreateFileContent()
{
    var sb = new StringBuilder();
    for (var i = 0; i < 100000; i++)
    {
        sb.AppendFormat("{0}", new Random(i).Next(0, 99999));
        sb.AppendLine();
    }
    return sb.ToString();
}

private static Task SimulateAsynchronousDelete(string fileName)
{
    // No delete async in API
    return Task.Run(() => File.Delete(fileName));
```

```
    }

    private static void Main(string[] args)
    {
      var t = ProcessAsynchronousIO();
      t.GetAwaiter().GetResult();
    }
```

When we run the code, we will see that only the numbers two and three writes are asynchronous. However, we have used the `await` statement and call `WriteAsync` in all cases. What is going on? The answer is that if we do not specify the correct options for the file API we use, the file will provide us with the wrong kind of asynchrony that uses worker threads for the I/O process and thus is not scalable.

This problem can be illustrated by the `SimulateAsynchronousDelete` method. There is no asynchronous delete function in the Win32 API, so it just starts a new task where the synchronous delete is being performed. This practice is called **async over sync** and should be avoided. Do not write your libraries like this. If there is no asynchronous API for some operation, do not make it look asynchronous. In the following diagram, we can see why it is a bad practice for a server application:

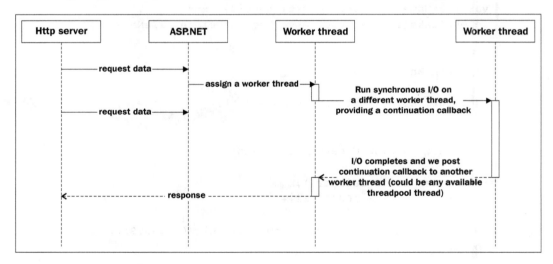

This workflow is even worse than the usual synchronous code, because there is an additional performance overhead related to running this part of the operation on a different worker thread. We end up wasting worker thread for the entire time of the I/O operation anyway, and this is fake asynchronous I/O. It is actually a CPU-bound operation that will affect the scalability and performance of your application.

So if we have the source code of a library, we can make sure that it leverages a truly asynchronous I/O. However, a source code is not always available, and even if it is available, it can often be puzzling and complicated. To make sure that our asynchrony is right, we can use a tool that shows the API calls from the application, and we will be able to see whether an I/O completion port has been used.

There is a program called API Monitor. It can be easily found in any search engine, is free to use, and easy to install. There are two versions of this program: 32-bit and 64-bit, so you have to pay attention to which version is appropriate for your application.

From the start, we will need to set up a filter to see only the required function calls. For our sample code, it is enough to monitor two functions, `CreateFileW` and `CreateIoCompletionPort`. The filter is shown in the following screenshot:

Then we need to run our application under API Monitor. To start monitoring, press *Ctrl + M* or use the **File | Monitor New Process...** menu option. The start dialog will appear as follows:

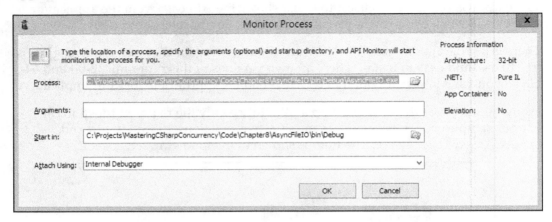

When you press **OK**, the application will start and then you will see a report as follows:

You can see that to write the `test2.txt` file, the `FILE_FLAG_OVERLAPPED` flag was provided to the `CreateFileW` function, meaning that we are using the I/O completion port. The `CreateFileW` function returned the `0x234` file handle, which was bound to the I/O completion port by calling the `CreateIoCompletionPort` function. The first and the last file writes are not using the completion port and thus are not really asynchronous.

Synchronization context

Another very important concept is synchronization context. We will review synchronization context and other kinds of context in detail in the next chapter, but for now let's start with a demonstration. This sample is called **IISSynchronizationContext**. This time we need to host our application in an IIS web server, so we will use the **Microsoft.Owin.Host.SystemWeb** NuGet package, and create an empty ASP.NET application. First, we will configure our application and define a default route:

```
public class Startup
{
  public void Configuration(IAppBuilder appBuilder)
  {
    var config = new HttpConfiguration();
    config.Routes.MapHttpRoute(
      "DefaultApi", "api/{controller}/{action}/{id}",
        new { id = RouteParameter.Optional}
      );

    appBuilder.UseWebApi(config);
  }
}
```

Then we will create a controller with two methods. One of them tries to get asynchronous operation results synchronously, and the other uses `await` and asynchronous execution:

```
public class HomeController : ApiController
{
  [HttpGet]
  public int Sync()
  {
    var lib = new AsyncLib();

    return lib.CountCharactersAsync(new
      Uri("http://google.com")).Result;
```

```
    }

    [HttpGet]
    public async Task<int> Async()
    {
      var lib = new AsyncLib();

      return await lib.CountCharactersAsync(new
        Uri("http://google.com"));
    }
}
```

Here we have defined our asynchronous operation as downloading content from a given URL and returning its length in characters:

```
public class AsyncLib
{
  public async Task<int> CountCharactersAsync(Uri uri)
  {
    using (var client = new HttpClient())
    {
      var content = await client.GetStringAsync(uri)
//    .ConfigureAwait(continueOnCapturedContext: false);

      return content.Length;
    }
  }
}
```

When we run this code in Visual Studio, a default web browser should start and open the web application URL. In the sample code, both actions can be reached via `http://localhost:5098/api/Home/Async` and `http://localhost:5098/api/Home/Sync` respectively. The `Async` version works fine, while the `Sync` code hangs forever.

This can be fixed if we uncomment the `ConfigureAwait` line in the `AsyncLib` class. If you run a new code, the `Sync` version will also work. To understand the reasons for this, we need to get back to the synchronization context concept. A synchronization context represents an environment that has some data associated to it, and an ability to run a delegate using this environment. In ASP.NET, when using a IIS web server there is a special synchronization context that keeps the current culture and user identity.

Now when we use await by default, if we use await with the Task<T> instance, we will get a special TaskAwaiter<T> structure that is used by the C# compiler in the generated state machine code. To run a continuation callback, C# ends up calling the UnsafeOnCompleted method:

```
public struct TaskAwaiter<TResult> : ICriticalNotifyCompletion
{
  private readonly Task<TResult> m_task;

  internal TaskAwaiter(Task<TResult> task)
  {
    Contract.Requires(task != null, "Constructing an awaiter
      requires a task to await.");
    m_task = task;
  }

  public void UnsafeOnCompleted(Action continuation)
  {
    TaskAwaiter.OnCompletedInternal(m_task, continuation,
      continueOnCapturedContext:true, flowExecutionContext:false);
  }
}
```

So this code tries to post a continuation callback to the current synchronization context. However when we run this code synchronously, we will get a classic deadlock situation:

- The code blocks the current synchronization context until the operation completes
- The operation completes and posts the continuation callback to the current synchronization context
- However, it is blocked until we get a result and cannot run this continuation callback, and thus cannot get a result
- All this leads to a deadlock

To prevent this, we can use the ConfigureAwait(continueOnCapturedContext: false) method. It returns a special ConfiguredTaskAwaitable type instance, which in turn returns ConfiguredTaskAwaiter to the C# compiler-generated code. In this case, we use UnsafeOnCompleted as well, but this time it is specifically configured not to capture the current synchronization context, and the continuation callback gets posted to a default task scheduler, which is likely to be a thread pool worker thread:

```
public struct ConfiguredTaskAwaiter : ICriticalNotifyCompletion
{
  private readonly Task<TResult> m_task;
```

```
private readonly bool m_continueOnCapturedContext;

internal ConfiguredTaskAwaiter(Task<TResult> task, bool
  continueOnCapturedContext)
{
  Contract.Requires(task != null, "Constructing an awaiter
    requires a task to await.");
  m_task = task;
  m_continueOnCapturedContext = continueOnCapturedContext;
}

public void UnsafeOnCompleted(Action continuation)
{
  OnCompletedInternal(m_task, continuation,
    m_continueOnCapturedContext, flowExecutionContext:false);
}
}
```

This means that when you write a library with async methods that have the `await` statements inside and if you are sure that your continuation code does not need the current synchronization context, always use `.ConfigureAwait(false)` to prevent such situations. Also vice versa; if you have to work with asynchronous operations synchronously in ASP.NET, it is very dangerous to use the `Task.Result` property and block the current thread. You should use `Task.ContinueWith` along with the corresponding options to get the result without `await`.

CPU-bound tasks and queues

So far, we have reviewed many special details about I/O-bound tasks, but what about CPU-bound work? Technically, the most efficient way will be to run such work synchronously and scale horizontally by adding more and more servers to be able to handle increasing load. Nevertheless, it can happen that this CPU-bound work is not the only responsibility of a server application. In this case, we can find a way to get this to work out of the web application, allowing it to run fast; now the CPU-bound part can be scaled separately and does not affect the rest of this application.

This is how cloud applications work. Usually, if there is a long running operation, a web application registers it into some data store, returns a unique identifier of this operation to the client, and posts this operation to a special queue. Then there is a separate pool of worker processes that monitor this queue, get tasks from them, process them, and write results to a data store. When the client arrives next time, the web application checks whether the task has been already completed by any worker and if it has, the application returns the result to the client.

Summary

In this chapter, we have learned about server applications and how they are different. We have looked at scalability and understood why it is very important for a server application to be able to scale well. We have created an OWIN Web API application and learned to host it in an IIS web server and in a separate process. We have used Visual Studio to create load tests for our server application, checked what happens when we use good and poorly written asynchronous code, and leveraged the Apache bench command line tool to run benchmarks without Visual Studio.

We also have reviewed in detail what an I/O thread and an I/O completion port are, and found out reasons why using an asynchronous I/O is the key to building scalable server applications. To check whether a third-party code uses real asynchronous I/O, we have found a tool that shows Win32 API calls. In conclusion, we have learned about synchronization context and how we can configure continuation tasks to be run on a default task scheduler. Finally, we have discussed how to enhance the scalability of a server application that has long-running CPU-bound tasks.

In the next chapter, we will review client applications, and specifically the user interface part, in detail. We will learn about modern user interface technologies, how to keep the UI fast and responsive, and how to avoid common pitfalls and mistakes with asynchrony on the client side.

Concurrency in the User Interface

9

In this chapter, we will review the aspects of using asynchrony in client applications. We will learn about how a Windows application works and define what an UI thread and message loop is. While going through the details of execution and synchronization contexts, we will dig into a C# compiler-generated code and see how it is related to the use of the `await` keyword in your program.

The importance of asynchrony for UI

While a server application in general has to be scalable before everything else, a client application is different. It is usually intended to run for one user on one computer, and thus the user expects it to run fast and not cause troubles for the other applications running in the system. While the second part is usually handled by the operating system, the application's performance in getting things done and reacting to user input is crucial for a positive user experience. Imagine if you run an application and it hangs for a few minutes after you click on a button. A good application remains responsive and indicates that you have just started a long-running operation that is still running and is going to complete soon. Meanwhile, you can do something else—click on other buttons and perform some other tasks. When the task is completed, you can get back to it and see the result.

However, achieving just this is often not enough. If you use some application and it reacts to your input even with a slight delay, it will be still very annoying. It is human nature to expect an immediate reaction, and even small delays can cause irritation and anger. This requires a program to offload work from the UI as much as possible, and for this we have to learn how the UI works and the UI threading architecture. Later in this chapter, we will go deeper into the details.

The last aspect is not relevant to this chapter, but is still very important. While a server application has to consume as few resources per user as possible, if your program needs computational power then it has to be able to use the necessary resources. For instance, if a user's computer has four core CPUs with **hyperthreading** technology, then the application has to be able to use all the logical cores to get the result as soon as possible. This is where this book's content will be very useful, especially *Chapter 7, Leveraging Parallel Patterns*, which provides you with concurrent programming patterns.

UI threads and message loops

Modern UI framework and programming languages not only make client application development much easier than before, but they also raise a level of abstraction and hide important implementation details. To understand how the UI works, we should look at the lower-level code.

The following is the code of a simple win32 program, which is written in C. If your Visual Studio does not have C/C++ project support installed, it is not a problem. This code is needed just to illustrate how a Windows application works, and we'll break it into parts and examine each part in detail. First, let's look at the full program code listing:

```c
#include <windows.h>

const char _szClassName[] = "ConcurrencyInUIWindowClass";

LRESULT CALLBACK WndProc(HWND hwnd, UINT msg, WPARAM wParam, LPARAM
lParam)
{
  switch (msg)
  {
  case WM_CLOSE:
    DestroyWindow(hwnd);
    break;
  case WM_DESTROY:
    PostQuitMessage(0);
    break;
  default:
    return DefWindowProc(hwnd, msg, wParam, lParam);
  }
  return 0;
}

int WINAPI WinMain(HINSTANCE hInstance, HINSTANCE hPrevInstance, LPSTR
lpCmdLine, int nCmdShow)
```

```
{
  WNDCLASSEX wc;
  HWND hwnd;
  MSG msg;

  // Creating the Window class
  wc.cbSize = sizeof(WNDCLASSEX);// size of the instance
  wc.style = 0;                  // class styles, not important here
  wc.lpfnWndProc = WndProc;      // the pointer to Window procedure
  wc.cbClsExtra = 0;             // extra data for this class
  wc.cbWndExtra = 0;             // extra data for this Window
  wc.hInstance = hInstance;      // application instance handle

  wc.hIcon = LoadIcon(NULL, IDI_APPLICATION);// standard large
                                             // icon
  wc.hCursor = LoadCursor(NULL, IDC_ARROW);  // standard arrow
                                             // cursor
  wc.hbrBackground = (HBRUSH)(COLOR_WINDOW + 1);// background
                                                // brush
  wc.lpszMenuName = NULL;          // name of menu resource
  wc.lpszClassName = _szClassName; // Window class name
  wc.hIconSm = LoadIcon(NULL, IDI_APPLICATION); // standard small
                                                //icon

  if (!RegisterClassEx(&wc))
  {
    MessageBox(NULL, "Window class registration failed!",
"Error!", MB_ICONEXCLAMATION | MB_OK);

    return 0;
  }

  hwnd = CreateWindowEx(
    WS_EX_CLIENTEDGE,
    _szClassName,
    "UI Concurrency",
    WS_OVERLAPPEDWINDOW,
    CW_USEDEFAULT, CW_USEDEFAULT, 480, 240,
    NULL, NULL, hInstance, NULL);

  if (hwnd == NULL)
  {
    MessageBox(NULL, "Window creation failed!",
    "Error!", MB_ICONEXCLAMATION | MB_OK);
```

```
    return 0;
}
ShowWindow(hwnd, nCmdShow);
UpdateWindow(hwnd);

while (GetMessage(&msg, NULL, 0, 0) > 0)
{
    TranslateMessage(&msg);
    DispatchMessage(&msg);
}

return msg.wParam;
}
```

The entry point is the WinMain method, which is a general entrance point for all Windows applications. This is what will be called when the application starts. This method is quite big, but basically it consists of four main steps.

The first step is to create the Window class instance, and provide it with the data required. The most important part here is the pointer to the Window procedure. In our case, it is the WndProc method, and it will be used later to process messages from the operating system. Also, we need a unique string name for our Window class to use it to create a window in our application.

The second step begins where the RegisterClassEx method is called. We register the Window class and immediately use its name to create the main application window using the CreateWindowEx function call. This call returns a handle that is needed for almost every operation related to this window. Then we display the application window on the screen using the ShowWindow and UpdateWindow methods.

The third step is very important and even highlighted in the code listing. This is what is usually called **the message loop** or **the message pump**. This cycle calls the GetMessage method that gets the first message from the message queue. This queue is created when a thread creates at least one window and thus becomes **the UI thread**. If the message queue is empty, the GetMessage method call gets blocked until any messages appear and it dequeues the first message. The operating system puts messages such as a key press or a mouse click on this queue, and then this message gets some preprocessing by the TranslateMessage function. Then DispatchMessage sends this message to the Window procedure that is appointed to the Window class that we have used to create the main application window. In our case it is the WndProc method, and it is responsible for reacting to the operating system and the application events. When the GetMessage method returns a result that is less than zero, the message loop stops and the application exits.

So the final step, that is step four, is the message processing inside `WndProc`. This has four parameters: `hwnd` is the Window handle and allows you to interact with the window, `msg` is the message id, and `wParam` and `lParam` contain specific data for each system message. In our Window procedure, we handle the `WM_CLOSE` and `WM_DESTROY` messages explicitly to show an example of message handling, and by default, we pass all messages to a standard message handler. If we run the application, we will see that it shows the empty application window with the custom title.

Now let's add the code to show a simple button click handler that will start an asynchronous operation. This code replaces the WndProc definition from the preceding code listing:

```
const UINT IDC_START_BUTTON = 101;
const UINT WM_ASYNC_TASK_COMPLETED = WM_USER + 0;

DWORD WINAPI SimulateAsyncOperation(LPVOID lpHwnd)
{
  // pretending that this is an async operation
  // posts the message to the UI message loop
  // from other thread
  HWND hwnd = *((HWND *)lpHwnd);
  Sleep(10000);
  SendMessage(hwnd, WM_ASYNC_TASK_COMPLETED, NULL, NULL);
  return 0;
}

LRESULT CALLBACK WndProc(HWND hwnd, UINT msg, WPARAM wParam,
  LPARAM lParam)
{
  switch (msg)
  {
  case WM_CREATE:
    {
      HGDIOBJ hfDefault = GetStockObject(DEFAULT_GUI_FONT);
      HWND hWndButton = CreateWindowEx(NULL,
        "BUTTON",
        "OK",
        WS_TABSTOP | WS_VISIBLE |
        WS_CHILD | BS_DEFPUSHBUTTON,
        50,
        80,
        100,
        24,
        hwnd,
```

```
                (HMENU) IDC_START_BUTTON,
                GetModuleHandle(NULL),
                NULL);
            SendMessage(hWndButton,
                WM_SETFONT,
                (WPARAM)hfDefault,
                MAKELPARAM(FALSE, 0));
        }
        break;
    case WM_COMMAND:
        switch (LOWORD(wParam))
        {
            case IDC_START_BUTTON:
                {
                    HANDLE threadHandle = CreateThread(NULL, 0,
                        SimulateAsyncOperation,
                        &hwnd, 0, NULL);
                    // we do not need the handle, so just close it
                    CloseHandle(threadHandle);

                    MessageBox(hwnd,
                        "Start button pressed",
                        "Information",
                        MB_ICONINFORMATION);
                }
                break;
        }
        break;
    case WM_ASYNC_TASK_COMPLETED:
        MessageBox(hwnd,
            "Operation completed",
            "Information",
            MB_ICONINFORMATION);
        break;

    case WM_CLOSE:
        // sends WM_DESTROY
        DestroyWindow(hwnd);
        break;
    case WM_DESTROY:
// Window cleanup here
        PostQuitMessage(0);
        break;
    default:
```

```
    return DefWindowProc(hwnd, msg, wParam, lParam);
    }
    return 0;
}
```

In the beginning, we have created identifiers for a button and a custom message. The details are not relevant here; they are just some numeric identifiers. The next part is an asynchronous operation code inside the SimulateAsyncOperation method. It just blocks the current thread for 5 seconds and then sends a custom message to the Window handle that it gets through the input parameter.

The remaining code is placed inside message handlers in the WndProc Window procedure. The first important place is the WM_CREATE message handler. Here we created a button, and set the button text font to a default system font. The other details are not important here; just notice the use of IDC_START_BUTTON inside the CreateWindowEx method call. This identifier will be used later in the message that the operating system will send when this button is clicked. This message will be processed by the WM_COMMAND message handler. The sending element identifier is passed in a low-order word of the wParam value. In the case of our button click, this value will be IDC_START_BUTTON. We can think of this like the common Button_Click handler in higher-level frameworks such as Windows Forms or WPF. Inside this button click handler, we have created a separate thread that will run the SimulateAsyncOperation method. Then the simplest solution is to show a modal message box showing that the operation has been started.

The last, but not the least, step is how we run continuation code after the asynchronous operation completes. The operation sends a custom message, and we handle it with the WM_ASYNC_TASK_COMPLETED message handler. It simply shows a message box informing about that the operation has been completed. The operation takes 10 seconds to complete, so you can close the first message box and drag around the application window to make sure that it stays responsive.

Of course, if we run SimulateAsyncOperation on the UI thread, it will freeze. Simply replace the button click handler code with this to make sure this really happens:

```
case IDC_START_BUTTON:
{
    MessageBox(hwnd,
      "Start button pressed",
      "Information",
      MB_ICONINFORMATION);

    SimulateAsyncOperation(&hwnd);
}
break;
```

Now if we run the code with these changes, the application window will stop responding for 10 seconds after we press the button and close the modal dialog. This perfectly illustrates what we are trying to achieve; do all the work on the other threads, leave the UI thread just to handle messages as fast as possible, and you will get a great and responsive UI in your application.

However, in modern UI programming, the abstraction level is very high, and usually you cannot be sure if some code runs on the UI thread or not just by looking at it. Consider this C# code that can be a part of any WPF application:

```
private static async void Click(object sender, EventArgs e)
{
  MessageBox.Show("Starting asynchronous operation....");

  await SomeOperationAsync();

  MessageBox.Show("Asynchronous operation complete!");
}
```

This is a button click handler that logically does the same thing as the previous code—shows a dialog, runs an asynchronous operation, and notifies us with message boxes about the start and end of the operation. It is much simpler than the native Win32 application window procedure message handling code. However, we pay the price by not knowing the details, and by just looking at this piece of code, we cannot say anything about what thread will run which part of this code.

Common problems and solutions

To see what can happen if we do not control how exactly the code correlates to threads, let's start with a simple WPF application that has three different buttons. In this particular case, it is not relevant how the WPF application gets created and how we compose UI controls, so we are going to concentrate on the code inside the button click handlers. All the code for this sample is located in the **AsyncInUI** project in the samples for **Chapter 9**. Besides this, we will not use `async` and `await` yet, because they will create one more abstraction level and thus make the code harder to understand.

The first button tries to call a `Task` returning method synchronously:

```
private static void SyncClick(object sender, EventArgs e)
{
    _label.Content = string.Empty;
    try
    {
```

```
        string result = TaskMethod().Result;

        _label.Content = result;
    }
    catch (Exception ex)
    {
        _label.Content = ex.Message;
    }
}
```

Without knowing exactly what `TaskMethod` is, it is impossible to predict how this program will behave. For now, we will experiment and only then look at its code and see what happened. If we run the application and click on the **Start synchronous operation** button, besides an unresponsive UI, we will get a weird error message:

One or more errors occurred

From *Chapter 5, C# Language Support for Asynchrony*, we already know that this is a message from the `AggregateException` instance. The easiest way to get the real exception message is by getting the `Task` result through the `GetAwaiter` method call. The new line of code will be:

```
    string result = TaskMethod().GetAwaiter().GetResult();
```

This time the UI gets blocked again, but we get the actual error message:

The calling thread cannot access this object because a different thread owns it.

This message tells us that we are trying to access a UI control from a non-UI thread, which is not allowed. Now is the time to dig into the `TaskMethod` code:

```
private static Task<string> TaskMethod()
{
    return TaskMethod(TaskScheduler.Default);
}

private static Task<string> TaskMethod(TaskScheduler scheduler)
{
  Task delay = Task.Delay(TimeSpan.FromSeconds(5));

  return delay.ContinueWith(t =>
  {
    string str = string.Format(
      "Task is running on a thread id {0}. Is thread pool
        thread: {1}", Thread.CurrentThread.ManagedThreadId,
          Thread.CurrentThread.IsThreadPoolThread);
```

```
      _label.Content = str;
      return str;
    },
    scheduler);
}
```

So we can see that we have created a timer task and then set up a continuation task using the default task scheduler, which tries to set the label text. Since the default task scheduler posts the task code to the thread pool, we get a multithreaded access error.

We have already covered task schedulers earlier in the book, and we know that we can get one for the current synchronization context. For now, let's say that this will allow us to post the code to the UI thread, and this would resolve the issue that we have. It seems that if we modify the code to use a proper task scheduler, we will get the required result:

```
string result = TaskMethod(
TaskScheduler.FromCurrentSynchronizationContext()).Result;
```

Unfortunately, if we run the modified program and press the button, the application will hang. The reason for this will become clear when we get back to the WndProc Window procedure source code. We will make a blocking call to TaskMethod from the button click handler, waiting for the asynchronous operation to complete. However, the button click handler runs on the UI thread, so this stops the message loop from spinning and therefore, we will never get a message from the asynchronous operation because the message loop cannot process the message as it is stopped. It is a classic deadlock situation and shows that using synchronous calls on tasks on the UI thread is quite dangerous.

Nevertheless, we can make this code work. WPF allows us to run the message loop manually:

```
public static class TaskExtensions
{
  public static T WaitWithNestedMessageLoop<T>(this Task<T> task)
  {
    var nested = new DispatcherFrame();
    task.ContinueWith(_ => nested.Continue = false,
      TaskScheduler.Default);

    Dispatcher.PushFrame(nested);
    return task.Result;
  }
}
```

This code creates a nested message loop. This means that the main message loop pauses, this one starts to process messages until we stop it, and then the main loop gets back in control. So first, we created the nested message loop. Then we set up a continuation task that is going to run on a thread pool worker thread. This task will stop the nested message loop when the initial task completes.

Finally, we started the nested message loop. The `PushFrame` method call is blocked until someone sets the `Continue` property on the message loop to false. The nested message loop will process system events and allow the UI to stay responsive while we wait for the initial task to complete. When this completes, the continuation task stops the nested message loop by setting its `Continue` property to `false`, and then we will get the task result (which will not block now, because the task has been completed) and return it.

Now, let's change the code and run it:

```
string result = TaskMethod(
TaskScheduler.FromCurrentSynchronizationContext())
.WaitWithNestedMessageLoop();
```

The UI stays responsive, and we get a message about the code that works while a label control runs on the UI thread, which is exactly what we wanted to achieve.

An asynchronous code, however, will work fine, because it does not block the UI thread and the message loop. To prove this, let's try to run asynchronous operations on the thread pool and on the UI thread:

```
private static void AsyncClick(object sender, EventArgs e)
{
  _label.Content = string.Empty;
  Mouse.OverrideCursor = Cursors.Wait;
  Task<string> task = TaskMethod();

  task.ContinueWith(t =>
    {
      _label.Content = t.Exception.InnerException.Message;
      Mouse.OverrideCursor = null;
    },
    CancellationToken.None,
    TaskContinuationOptions.OnlyOnFaulted,
    TaskScheduler.FromCurrentSynchronizationContext()
  );
}

private static void AsyncOkClick(object sender, EventArgs e)
```

```
  {
    _label.Content = string.Empty;
    Mouse.OverrideCursor = Cursors.Wait;
    Task<string> task = TaskMethod(
      TaskScheduler.FromCurrentSynchronizationContext());

    task.ContinueWith(t => Mouse.OverrideCursor = null,
      CancellationToken.None,
      TaskContinuationOptions.None,
      TaskScheduler.FromCurrentSynchronizationContext());
  }
```

Since we did not want to use await here, we have to set up continuation tasks to output the result. In the AsyncClick method, we know that the asynchronous call is going to fail, so we set up an error handling continuation task using the UI thread task scheduler. In the second case, everything is going to be fine, so the continuation task will show a success message. Running the program and clicking on the second and third buttons proves our assumptions.

How the await keyword works

Now let's write a button click handler using await and see what has changed:

```
private static async void Click(object sender, EventArgs e)
{
  _label.Content = "Starting asynchronous operation....";

  await SomeOperationAsync();

  _label.Content = "Asynchronous operation complete!";
}
```

Once again, without knowing exactly what SomeOperationAsync is, it is still impossible to know how this code is going to behave. Imagine the simplest asynchronous method implementation:

```
static Task SomeOperationAsync()
{
  return Task.Delay(TimeSpan.FromSeconds(5));
}
```

In this case, the program will run successfully, which means that the continuation code runs on the UI thread. To find out how this happens, we need to review two important abstractions: execution and synchronization contexts.

Execution and synchronization contexts

An **execution context** contains all the data related to the current environment in which a thread is running. Usually, there is no need to use this directly; it is used by the framework to contain the thread's local information such as security information. When needed, it is possible to restore this information to another thread. the C# infrastructure captures the execution context and flows it into a continuation code by default.

Here is an example of the code generated by the C# compiler to perform an asynchronous method call with `await`:

```
public AsyncVoidMethodBuilder <>t__builder;
...
TaskAwaiter awaiter = Program.SomeOperationAsync().GetAwaiter();
...
// in case the operation is not completed yet
this.<>__builder.AwaitUnsafeOnCompleted(ref awaiter, ref this);
```

So if we look at the `AsyncVoidMethodBuilder.AwaitUnsafeOnCompleted` method, it will contain the following code:

```
[SecuritySafeCritical]
public void AwaitUnsafeOnCompleted<TAwaiter, TStateMachine>(
  ref TAwaiter awaiter, ref TStateMachine stateMachine)
where TAwaiter : ICriticalNotifyCompletion
where TStateMachine : IAsyncStateMachine
{
  try
  {
    var continuation = m_coreState
    .GetCompletionAction(ref this, ref stateMachine);

    Contract.Assert(continuation != null,
    "GetCompletionAction should always return a valid action.");

    awaiter.UnsafeOnCompleted(continuation);
  }
  catch (Exception e)
  {
    AsyncMethodBuilderCore.ThrowAsync(e, targetContext: null);
  }
}
```

Now, we get a continuation delegate by calling the `GetCompletionAction` method:

```
internal Action GetCompletionAction<TMethodBuilder,
  TStateMachine>(
  ref TMethodBuilder builder, ref TStateMachine stateMachine)
  where TMethodBuilder : IAsyncMethodBuilder
  where TStateMachine : IAsyncStateMachine
  {
  . . .

    // The builder needs to flow ExecutionContext, so capture it.
    var capturedContext = ExecutionContext.FastCapture();

  . . .
  }
```

So, we capture the current synchronization context and use it to run a continuation code.

Synchronization context is another concept that abstracts away the implementation details of some environment that is able to run the code. It can be a Windows Forms environment that runs a delegate with the help of the `Control.BeginInvoke` method, a WPF environment that can run the code using the `Dispatcher` object, or just any other framework that needs such an environment to run the code.

Let's look at the preceding code, specifically at the `awaiter.UnsafeOnCompleted(continuation)` part. The C# async infrastructure uses the `TaskAwaiter` type for the `awaiter` variable, which has the following `UnsafeOnCompleted` method:

```
[SecurityCritical]
public void UnsafeOnCompleted(Action continuation)
{
  TaskAwaiter.OnCompletedInternal(m_task,
    continuation,
    continueOnCapturedContext:true,
    flowExecutionContext:false);
}
```

You can see that we captured the current synchronization context. However, notice that the `flowExecutionContext` parameter is set to **false**. This only means that the execution context flow happens in another place in the code; here we are only capturing the current synchronization context.

Well, now we understand how the C# asynchronous infrastructure makes the current execution and synchronization contexts run a continuation code. Is it possible to change this behavior? The answer is yes, it is possible. To stop capturing the current synchronization context, we can use the special `ConfigureAwait` method on the `Task` instance:

```
private static async void Click(object sender, EventArgs e)
{
  _label.Content = "Starting asynchronous operation....";

  await SomeOperationAsync()
  .ConfigureAwait(continueOnCapturedContext: false);

  _label.Content = "Asynchronous operation complete!";
}
```

Using the `ConfigureAwait` method will lead to another awaiter type, `ConfiguredTaskAwaiter`. This will be used by the C# asynchronous infrastructure. It implements `UnsafeOnCompleted` slightly differently:

```
[SecurityCritical]
public void UnsafeOnCompleted(Action continuation)
{
  TaskAwaiter.OnCompletedInternal(m_task,
    continuation,
    m_continueOnCapturedContext,
    flowExecutionContext: false);
}
```

We can see that providing **false** to the `ConfigureAwait` method will cause the synchronization context to not be captured. If we run the modified application and press the button, we will get a multithreaded UI control access exception.

Performance issues

So far, we have only observed problems related to multithreaded access to the UI controls. By default, the C# `await` statement will use the current synchronization and execution contexts and post the continuation code to the appropriate environment. Is there any use for the `ConfigureAwait` method? Why should we ever try to change the default behavior? To answer this question, consider the following application. This time we will review the whole code including the one that assembles the application:

```
private static Label _label;

[STAThread]
static void Main(string[] args)
```

```
    {
        var app = new Application();
        var win = new Window();
        var panel = new StackPanel();
        var button = new Button();
        _label = new Label();
        _label.FontSize = 32;
        _label.Height = 200;
        button.Height = 100;
        button.FontSize = 32;
        button.Content = "Start asynchronous operations";
        button.Click += Click;
        panel.Children.Add(_label);
        panel.Children.Add(button);
        win.Content = panel;
        app.Run(win);

        Console.ReadLine();
    }
```

A thread where we create the UI controls must be a **Single-Threaded Apartment** thread, or **STA**. This term comes from Component Object Model (**COM**) and is basically required for the UI message loop to be able to interact with COM components. Many OS components, such as system dialogs, use this technology. To make things easier, just remember that the UI thread in .NET and Windows must be marked by the STAThread attribute.

Then, we create several UI controls, compose them in the object model, and finally app.Run(win) shows the application window and starts its message loop:

```
    async static void Click(object sender, EventArgs e)
    {
        _label.Content = "Calculating...";
        TimeSpan resultWithContext = await Test();
        TimeSpan resultNoContext = await TestNoContext();
        var sb = new StringBuilder();
        sb.AppendLine(string.Format("With the context: {0}",
          resultWithContext));
        sb.AppendLine(string.Format("Without the context: {0}",
          resultNoContext));
        sb.AppendLine(string.Format("Ratio: {0:0.00}",
          resultWithContext.TotalMilliseconds /
            resultNoContext.TotalMilliseconds));

        _label.Content = sb.ToString();
    }
```

The button click handler does a very simple job. It runs two asynchronous operations, gets their results, and then outputs these results to the label control on the main application window. Since we use the `await` statement, we can work with the UI controls from the latter code.

Now to the most important part of this sample — asynchronous performance tests:

```
async static Task<TimeSpan> Test()
{
  const int iterationsNumber = 100000;
  var sw = new Stopwatch();
  sw.Start();
  for (int i = 0; i < iterationsNumber; i++)
  {
    var t = Task.Run(() => { });
    await t;
  }
  sw.Stop();
  return sw.Elapsed;
}

async static Task<TimeSpan> TestNoContext()
{
  const int iterationsNumber = 100000;
  var sw = new Stopwatch();
  sw.Start();
  for (int i = 0; i < iterationsNumber; i++)
  {
    var t = Task.Run(() => { });
    await t.ConfigureAwait(continueOnCapturedContext: false);
  }
  sw.Stop();
  return sw.Elapsed;
}
```

Both tests do almost the same thing. For a large number of iterations, they create a task, wait for its completion, and finally return the whole amount of time taken by the test to run. These two test codes are different only with respect to the `ConfigureAwait` method usage in the second test code. However, this subtle difference produces a huge performance effect.

If we run the program and press the button, we will see quite a noticeable difference between test performances. On a reference machine, the first test is about ten times slower than the second one. However, if you run the application again and then, after pressing the button, you start resizing or dragging the application window, you will notice that the first test becomes even slower. I managed to make it twelve times slower than the second test.

The answer is simple: the first test uses the UI thread to run a continuation code for each of the one hundred thousand iterations, thus posting the same number of messages on the UI message loop. When we resize or drag the main application window, we produce other messages in the UI that make the message loop run slower, and the test becomes slower as well. This is definitely not a good practice and should be controlled using the `ConfigureAwait` method call.

The second test uses the thread pool worker threads to post its continuation code. Since the thread pool is very well optimized for small, short-running tasks, we get good performance here.

 If you write a library code, always be careful to avoid the synchronization context. If your continuation code does not require this, always use `ConfigureAwait` to turn off the synchronization context flow.

After running the preceding code snippet, we get the following output:

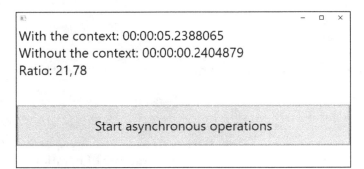

```
With the context: 00:00:05.2388065
Without the context: 00:00:00.2404879
Ratio: 21,78


                  Start asynchronous operations

```

Imagine that the first test is a third-party code and cannot be modified. Can we do anything about this? People often try to use `ConfigureAwait` as in the following example:

```
async static void Click(object sender, EventArgs e)
{
  _label.Content = "Calculating...";
```

```
var dispatcher = Dispatcher.CurrentDispatcher;

TimeSpan resultWithContext = await Test().ConfigureAwait(false);

TimeSpan resultNoContext = await TestNoContext();
var sb = new StringBuilder();
sb.AppendLine(string.Format("With the context: {0}",
  resultWithContext));
sb.AppendLine(string.Format("Without the context: {0}",
  resultNoContext));
sb.AppendLine(string.Format("Ratio: {0:0.00}",
  resultWithContext.TotalMilliseconds /
    resultNoContext.TotalMilliseconds));

dispatcher.Invoke( () =>
{
  _label.Content = sb.ToString();
});
}
```

Here we had to slightly modify the code to be able to work with the UI control from the thread pool worker thread. Be aware that if we use the `Dispatcher.CurrentDispatcher.Invoke` method to set the label text, the code will fail because all the highlighted code runs in a continuation of the first `await` statement, and thus runs on the thread pool. So, here we have to get a dispatcher reference before running the asynchronous code.

However, nothing has changed for the `Test` method itself. It still captures the current context and uses the UI thread to run all the iterations. To be able to fix the first test, we have to switch the synchronization context to the thread pool before we run this test. A simple workaround will look like this:

```
async static void Click(object sender, EventArgs e)
{
  _label.Content = "Calculating...";

  var dispatcher = Dispatcher.CurrentDispatcher;

  await Task.Delay(1).ConfigureAwait(false);

  TimeSpan resultWithContext = await Test();
  TimeSpan resultNoContext = await TestNoContext();
  var sb = new StringBuilder();
  sb.AppendLine(string.Format("With the context: {0}",
    resultWithContext));
```

```
    sb.AppendLine(string.Format("Without the context: {0}",
        resultNoContext));
    sb.AppendLine(string.Format("Ratio: {0:0.00}",
        resultWithContext.TotalMilliseconds /
            resultNoContext.TotalMilliseconds));

    dispatcher.Invoke( () =>
    {
        _label.Content = sb.ToString();
    });
}
```

Now the first test is inside the continuation code, which runs on the thread pool worker thread, and it uses the thread pool synchronization context. If we run the application, we will see that both tests perform more or less equally.

This trick can be very useful when dealing with poorly written third-party libraries. Unfortunately, usually such problems are very hard to notice at first glance, and you find them accidentally in the profiler while looking for the roots of some other problems.

After running the preceding code snippet, we get the following output:

With the context: 00:00:00.2437126
Without the context: 00:00:00.2432675
Ratio: 1,00

Start asynchronous operations

Summary

In this chapter, we have seen the implementation details of traditional Windows application UIs that are usually hidden by the programming platform and high-level UI frameworks. We have learned about what the UI thread and message loop are, and why they are very important to keep the UI thread running and not blocking it with long-running code. Then we learned about the common problems of asynchrony in the UI, and how to avoid deadlocks and multithreaded access to the UI controls' exceptions.

One of the most important topics covered in this chapter was the C# asynchronous infrastructure internals, showing how the `await` statement works, and how we can improve application performance by choosing not to keep the current synchronization context.

In the next chapter, we will look at troubleshooting concurrent programs in greater detail. We will know about many exciting features of Visual Studio for profiling and debugging parallel programs and find out how to catch more errors in the development stage with the help of unit and functional tests.

10
Troubleshooting Parallel Programs

This chapter is dedicated to parallel program debugging specifics. We will review how concurrent code is different, what additional problems we usually get, and what can be done to find and fix bugs effectively in multithreaded applications.

How troubleshooting parallel programs is different

A concurrent program like any usual program can contain programming errors that could lead to incorrect results. However, concurrency usually leads programs to become more complicated, causing errors to be trickier and harder to find. As mentioned in *Chapter 1, Traditional Concurrency*, there are typical problems related to concurrent shared state access — race conditions and deadlocks, but there are many other kinds of problems specific to concurrent programs. While we will not try to describe every kind of problem in detail, since it will take another book to do that, we will instead describe several techniques that allow us to detect and fix problems over the different stages of working with concurrent programs.

Heisenbugs

This is one more problem type, not strictly related to concurrent programming, but much more common with it, usually referred to as **heisenbug**. This term is defined in Wikipedia as follows:

> *In computer programming jargon, a heisenbug is a software bug that seems to disappear or alter its behaviour when one attempts to study it. The term is a pun on the name of Werner Heisenberg, the physicist who first asserted the observer effect of quantum mechanics, which states that the act of observing a system inevitably alters its state.*

These problems are usually extremely hard to reproduce and debug, since they usually appear in some special conditions such as high user load, or some specific events timing, and more. This is the kind of bug which you will inevitably meet while developing concurrent applications.

Besides what we have mentioned so far, concurrent programs can have problems related to infrastructure, such as synchronization contexts and UI, performance problems, or any other kind of problems, which are not related to concurrency and multithreading at all.

To make your program less error-prone, you have to use a combined approach that allows the finding and elimination of bugs in the different stages of developing your application from writing code to analyzing logs of production deployment. There are three main stages that are crucial to create robust and performant applications:

- **Writing tests**: This is a very important step that can dramatically reduce bugs in your code. With these tests, it is possible to detect problems right after writing the code, or after deploying your application into a test environment.

- **Debugging**: Visual Studio has specific features and tools to make debugging concurrent applications easier.

- **Performance measurement and profiling**: This is one more very important step that can help to detect whether your program spends too much time switching between threads or blocking them instead of doing its job.

Writing tests

Tests allow us to detect errors at the very early stages of development. They require significant investment in terms of time and effort, but in return they save a lot of time that could be later spent in debugging the application, which is always much harder. There are different kinds of tests that can help to detect different problems in the application.

Load tests

If your application has to deal with multiple concurrent users, it is likely that with the increase in the number of users, you will experience problems that cannot be revealed in normal conditions. Simulating a large user load and further log analysis, or studying profiling results is always a good idea and a powerful tool to detect potential pitfalls.

In *Chapter 8, Server-Side Asynchrony*, we reviewed a couple of ways to organize a load test. To simulate really large user activity, it could be not enough to use a single machine. It is possible to use Visual Studio Online to run a load test using the power of Microsoft Azure to run several virtual machines and use them all to create a test load for your application. You will need a Visual Studio Online account, and you will need to set a special flag in your test settings file:

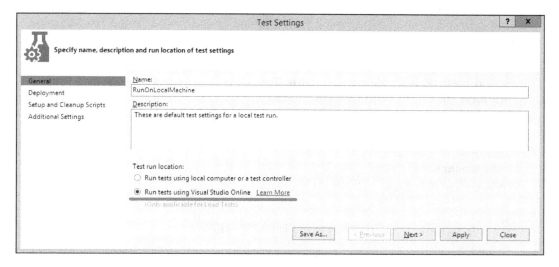

Unit tests

With unit tests, we can perform tests on small isolated parts of our code. For example, if we have an `AsyncCounter` class that contains some concurrent counter calculations. The first method contains a **race condition**, which leads to incorrect counter value calculation:

```
public async Task<int> CountWithRaceConditionAsync()
{
    const int iterations = 10000;
    var counter = 0;
    Action count =
        () =>
```

```
    {
      for (int i = 0; i < iterations; i++)
      {
        counter++;
        Thread.SpinWait(100);
        counter--;
      }
    };
  var tasks =
    Enumerable
      .Range(0, 8)
      .Select(n => Task.Run(count))
      .ToArray();

  await Task.WhenAll(tasks);

  return counter;
}
```

The second method is implemented using the `Interlocked` operations, and thus does not have problems with race conditions:

```
public async Task<int> CountWithInterlockedAsync()
{
  const int iterations = 10000;
  var counter = 0;
  Action count =
    () =>
    {
      for (int i = 0; i < iterations; i++)
      {
        Interlocked.Increment(ref counter);
        Thread.SpinWait(100);
        Interlocked.Decrement(ref counter);
      }
    };
  var tasks =
    Enumerable
      .Range(0, 8)
      .Select(n => Task.Run(count))
      .ToArray();

  await Task.WhenAll(tasks);

  return counter;
}
```

However, the first method can sometimes produce correct results, so an incorrect implementation can make its way into a production code. To prevent this from happening, let's write a test that runs calculations and checks their results. To write tests, we will use the standard Visual Studio unit test project and the Visual Studio Unit Testing Framework. The test to check these counters looks like this:

```
[TestClass]
public class CounterTests
{
  [TestMethod]
  public async Task TestCounterWithRaceCondition()
  {
    var counter = new AsyncCounter();
    int count = await counter.CountWithRaceConditionAsync();
    Assert.AreEqual(0, count);
  }

  [TestMethod]
  public async Task TestCounterWitInterlocked()
  {
    var counter = new AsyncCounter();
    int count = await counter.CountWithInterlockedAsync();
    Assert.AreEqual(0, count);
  }
}
```

Notice that the test methods are marked as **async** and returned as `Task`. This allows us to use **await** inside tests, and this is supported in all the major modern unit testing frameworks. The `TestClass` attribute informs the unit testing framework that this class contains unit tests, and `TestMethod` marks a single test.

To run tests, we navigate to the **Test | Run | All Tests...** menu option. Then you will see the Test Explorer window that shows the unit test results. The race condition unit test will fail, because we expect it to return 0, but due to the race condition it usually returns some other number. The other test will succeed:

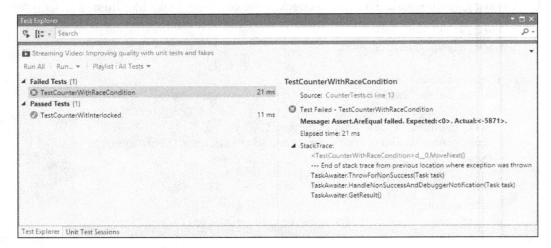

Now let's try to write a test that will detect deadlocks.

First, we will prepare another asynchronous library, `AsyncLib`, that contains two methods. The first method just waits for one second and completes successfully. The second one contains a code that intentionally simulates deadlock:

```
public class AsyncLib
{
  public async Task GoodMethodAsync()
  {
    await Task.Delay(TimeSpan.FromSeconds(1));
  }

  public async Task DeadlockMethodAsync()
  {
    var lock1 = new object();
    var lock2 = new object();

    Task task1 = Task.Run(() =>
    {
      lock (lock1)
      {
        Thread.Sleep(200);
        lock (lock2)
```

```
          {
          }
        }
    });

    Task task2 = Task.Run(() =>
    {
      lock (lock2)
      {
        Thread.Sleep(200);
        lock (lock1)
        {
        }
      }
    });

    await Task.WhenAll(task1, task2);
  }
}
```

To detect a deadlock, we can only check whether an asynchronous method call completes before a certain timeout. We can add an extension method to `Task` that will help us to set the expected execution timeout value in milliseconds. After the timeout expires, we will get `TimeoutException` if the task is not completed:

```
public static class TaskExtensions
{
  public static async Task TimeoutAfter(this Task task,
    int millisecondsTimeout)
  {
    if (task == await Task.WhenAny(task,
      Task.Delay(millisecondsTimeout)))
    {
      await task;
    }
    else
    {
      throw new TimeoutException();
    }
  }
}
```

The unit test code will be very easy—we'll just add a `TimeoutAfter` method call to each asynchronous function:

```
[TestClass]
public class LockTests
{
  [TestMethod]
  public async Task TestGoodAsync()
  {
    var lib = new AsyncLib();
    await lib.GoodMethodAsync().TimeoutAfter(2000);
  }


  [TestMethod]
  public async Task TestDeadlockAsync()
  {
    var lib = new AsyncLib();
    await lib.DeadlockMethodAsync().TimeoutAfter(2000);
  }
}
```

As a result of running this test, we will see that we have detected a deadlock:

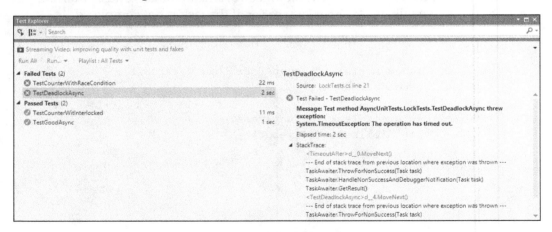

Visual Studio has an option to run unit tests after each build. This will make the build process slightly longer, but we will see that unit test fails are similar to compilation errors. This is very comfortable and helps to identify a problem as soon as we write the code. The Visual Studio 2013 Ultimate edition has a feature called **CodeLens** that will show unit test errors right beside the code related to the test:

Integration tests

A unit test is a very powerful concept that can increase product quality and can be used to find many bugs as soon as they appear in the code. However, when your application becomes more and more complicated, testing separate small components is not enough. Many problems appear when we use these components together, and while two asynchronous methods can run well separately, they can cause a deadlock while running simultaneously. This is why it is very important to write higher-level tests for your application that run the application's business logic altogether. Such tests are called integration tests because we check how the application components work together.

To illustrate this approach, we will take a slightly changed code from *Chapter 8, Server-Side Asynchrony*. This is an OWIN Web API application, and we will test this with an HTTP API controller:

```
public class HomeController : ApiController
{
  [HttpGet]
  public int Sync()
  {
    var lib = new AsyncHttp();
```

```
    return lib.CountCharactersAsync(new
      Uri("http://google.com")).Result;
  }

  [HttpGet]
  public async Task<int> Async()
  {
    var lib = new AsyncHttp();

    return await lib.CountCharactersAsync(new
      Uri("http://google.com"));
  }
}
```

This controller looks very simple. However, in a real application, controllers are usually the places that contain application logic, and controller actions call several application components and use the results to provide the client with the data needed. Here it is shown how to write an integration test for such a controller, so you can use this approach with your code.

Referring to *Chapter 8, Server-Side Asynchrony*, we remember that this controller has a problem. A synchronous call to an asynchronous method could result in a deadlock. So let's write a test that will look for a deadlock here. First, we will need to modify the `TimeoutAfter` extension method to deal with the parameterized `Task<T>` type. The easiest approach is to use the reactive extensions NuGet package. We will need to reference the **Reactive Extensions – Core Library** package. Then, we can write the following code:

```
public static Task<T> TimeoutAfter<T>(this Task<T> task,
  int millisecondsTimeout)
{
  return task.ToObservable().Timeout(
    TimeSpan.FromMilliseconds(millisecondsTimeout)).ToTask();
}
```

Then, we're going to write the test. First of all, we need to reference the OWIN Web API NuGet package. Then we need to add one more package, **Microsoft.Owin. Testing,** that hosts the whole OWIN application in memory. Then we will use the new `ClassInitialize` and `ClassCleanup` attributes to create a test server and get rid of it when the tests complete:

```
[TestClass]
public class ServerInMemoryTests
{
  private static TestServer _server;
  private static HttpClient _client;
```

```
[ClassInitialize]
public static void ClassInit(TestContext context)
{
  _server = TestServer.Create<Startup>();
  _client = _server.HttpClient;
}

[TestMethod]
public async Task TestSyncAction()
{
  var response = await _client.GetAsync("/api/Home/Sync")
.TimeoutAfter(2000);

  var result = await response.Content.ReadAsAsync<int>();

  Assert.IsTrue(result > 0);
}

[TestMethod]
public async Task TestAsyncAction()
{
  var response = await _client.GetAsync("/api/Home/Async")
.TimeoutAfter(2000);

  var result = await response.Content.ReadAsAsync<int>();

  Assert.IsTrue(result > 0);
}

[ClassCleanup]
public static void ClassCleanup()
{
  _server.Dispose();
}
}
```

This test establishes the OWIN pipeline in memory and uses a regular HttpClient class to simulate http calls to HomeController by expecting to get a greater than zero number.

However, when we run this test, we are going to find out that everything is fine and no deadlock will be found:

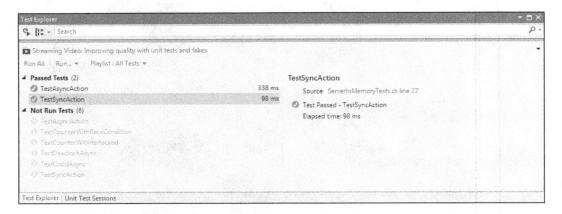

The reason why there is no deadlock here is that the deadlock was related to the synchronization context in the ASP.NET environment, and this test used in-memory hosting. However, we can detect here any application component's interaction issues, and this kind of test is also good to run after each build in Visual Studio.

To detect infrastructure issues, we have to test the application by running it in the same environment that will be used in production. Fortunately, this is quite easy to do. Instead of creating an in-memory host, we just need to run our application and slightly modify the test code to use a real http interaction:

```
[TestClass]
public class ServerHttpTests
{
  private static HttpClient _client;

  [ClassInitialize]
  public static void ClassInit(TestContext context)
  {
    _client = new HttpClient();
    _client.BaseAddress = new Uri("http://localhost:1845/");
  }

  [TestMethod]
  public async Task TestSyncAction()
  {
    var response = await _client.GetAsync("/api/Home/Sync")
.TimeoutAfter(2000);
```

```
      var result = await response.Content.ReadAsAsync<int>();

      Assert.IsTrue(result > 0);
    }

    [TestMethod]
    public async Task TestAsyncAction()
    {
      var response = await _client.GetAsync("/api/Home/Async")
  .TimeoutAfter(2000);
      var result = await response.Content.ReadAsAsync<int>();

      Assert.IsTrue(result > 0);
    }

    [ClassCleanup]
    public static void ClassCleanup()
    {
      _client.Dispose();
    }
  }
```

Notice that the test code remains the same. We have only changed the `HttpClient` instance. Here we just point it to our application URL, and this is all that we have changed. Now the test detects a deadlock where we expected it to occur:

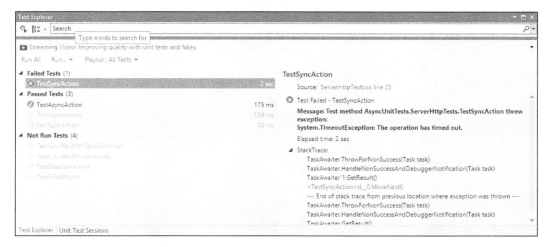

This kind of test is not intended to be run along with the built-in Visual Studio. The proper place to run these tests is your continuous integration process, when you create a new build on your build server, deploy the application into a test environment, configure it and pre-populate data storage with some test data, and then run a test suite on this application instance.

> The testing stage is very important, because it is much harder to find problems in the debugging or profiling stage. Investing in tests can help to save a lot of further efforts to find out what is wrong with the application, and greatly reduce the number of problems that get into the production environment.

Debugging

Debugging as a very extensive topic and there are several books about debugging .NET applications techniques. Here we will review how we can start debugging with Visual Studio, and what tools can help us to debug concurrent applications.

Just my code setting

There is a very important setting located in the **Debug, Options and Settings...** menu called **Enable Just My Code**:

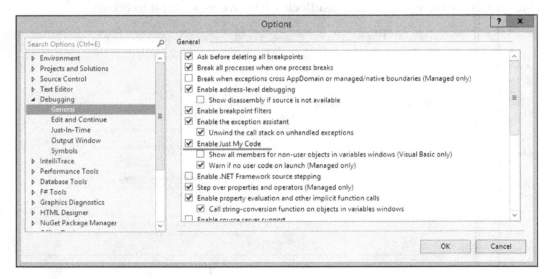

When this setting is enabled, Visual Studio tries to hide additional information such as compiler-generated code and does not show this in debugging windows, concentrating only on the information related to your code. This seems comfortable, but do not forget that you can always turn it off and study the whole picture in case you need to dig into the infrastructure code.

Call stack window

One of the easiest debugging tools in Visual Studio is the **call stack** window. An asynchronous method call usually consists of two parts—begin and end operation. If you have a breakpoint inside an asynchronous method body, it is not easy to find out where this operation has been initiated. Fortunately, if you have the latest Visual Studio 2013 installed at least on Windows 8.1 or Windows 2012R2, the call stack window will show you a full call stack including the asynchronous operation starting point.

We may run this code under the debugger, as follows:

```
class Program
{
  static void Main(string[] args)
  {
    StartAsyncOperation().GetAwaiter().GetResult();
  }

  public static async Task StartAsyncOperation()
  {
    Console.WriteLine("Starting async operation");
    await AsyncOperation();
    Console.WriteLine("After finishing async operation");
  }

  public static async Task AsyncOperation()
  {
    Console.WriteLine("Inside async operation");
    await Task.Delay(TimeSpan.FromSeconds(1));

    Console.WriteLine("Async operation complete!");
  }
}
```

In this case, we will see in the call stack window that the operation has been initiated in the StartAsyncOperation method:

Threads window

Another useful Visual Studio debugging feature is the **Threads** window. It shows the current threads in the application and allows us to suspend and resume any thread with corresponding buttons and filter threads by marking them with flags and pressing the double flag button:

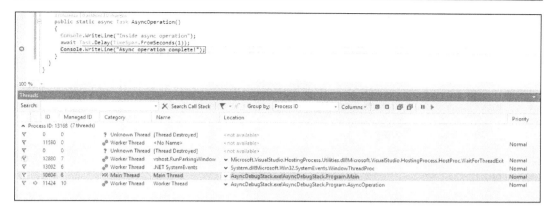

Tasks window

With the **Tasks** window, it is possible to review incomplete TPL tasks and see the different information about them:

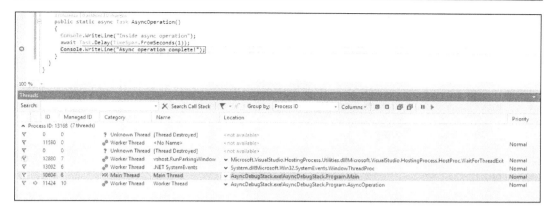

The **Tasks** window has deadlock diagnostics that inform us about tasks that are deadlocked. To see it in action, we have to run the following code until a deadlock occurs and then press the break button on the debugger toolbar:

```csharp
class Program
{
  static void Main(string[] args)
  {
    DeadlockMethodAsync().GetAwaiter().GetResult();
  }

  public static async Task DeadlockMethodAsync()
  {
    var lock1 = new object();
    var lock2 = new object();

    Task task1 = Task.Run(() =>
    {
      lock (lock1)
      {
        Thread.Sleep(200);
        lock (lock2)
        {
        }
      }
    });
    Task task2 = Task.Run(() =>
    {
      lock (lock2)
      {
        Thread.Sleep(200);
        Debugger.Break();
        lock (lock1)
        {
        }
      }
    });

    Debugger.Break();
    // here you can open Tasks window in Visual Studio
    await Task.WhenAll(task1, task2);
  }
}
```

Parallel stacks window

To visualize an asynchronous program flow, we can use the **Parallel Stacks** window. Let's run a simple parallel `foreach` loop:

```csharp
class Program
{
  static void Main(string[] args)
  {
    ParallelForEach().GetAwaiter().GetResult();
  }

  public static async Task ParallelForEach()
  {
    Parallel.ForEach(Enumerable.Range(0, 32), i =>
    {
      Console.WriteLine(i);
      if (i == 24)
      {
        Debugger.Break();
      }
      Thread.Sleep(new Random(i).Next(100, 500));
    });
  }
}
```

This screenshot has been made on a virtual machine with six core CPUs. We see that one of the tasks was scheduled to run on the main thread:

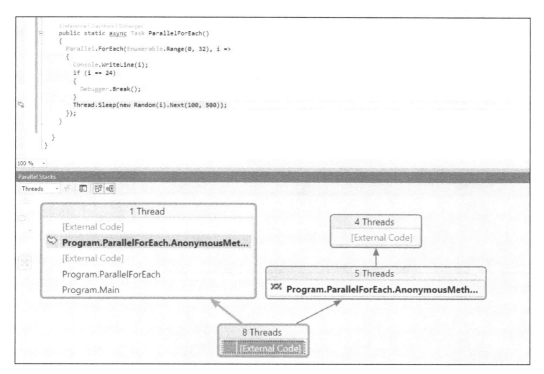

If we turn off the **Enable Just My Code** setting, we will see more details about how the concurrent program is organized.

Performance measurement and profiling

There is a profiler in Visual Studio that can be used to visualize concurrency in your application and see what is going on. Depending on the Visual Studio version, its behavior is different. In Visual Studio 2010, you would just run a profiler session collecting concurrency data and get the required result. In Visual Studio 2012, there was a separate menu option called **Concurrency Visualizer** and this is the most comfortable way to look at concurrency processes in your application.

In Visual Studio 2013, there is no Concurrency Visualizer option by default, and you can still use the regular profiler to collect the basic concurrency information. However, you can install Concurrency Visualizer separately.

The Concurrency Visualizer

The Concurrency Visualizer is available for Visual Studio 2013 as a separate extension. You can install it in Visual Studio:

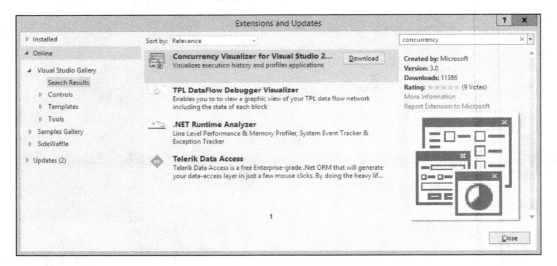

After the installation, you will get a **Concurrency Visualizer** menu option under the **Analyze** menu in Visual Studio:

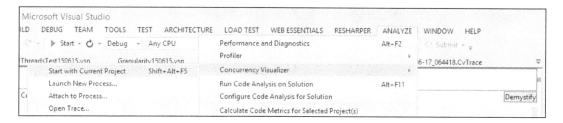

Concurrency Visualizer provides a lot of useful information. To illustrate this, let's compare the parallelism granularity test from *Chapter 3, Understanding Parallelism Granularity*, and I/O threads from *Chapter 8, Server-Side Asynchrony*. The first program under Concurrency Visualizer will look like this:

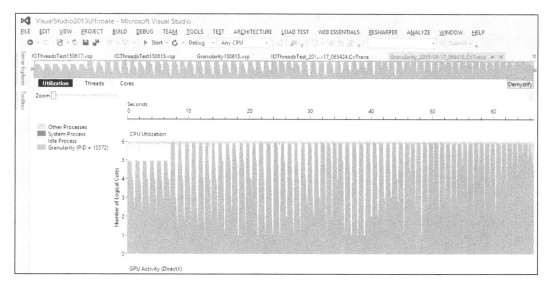

It can be clearly seen that the program consumes a lot of CPU resources. Now if we visualize I/O threads, we will see that it consumes almost no CPU resources:

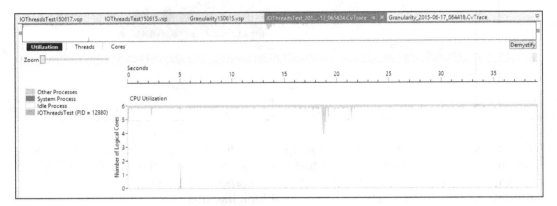

We can see more details if we go to the **Threads** tab inside the report. The granularity program shows a significant CPU load, as shown here:

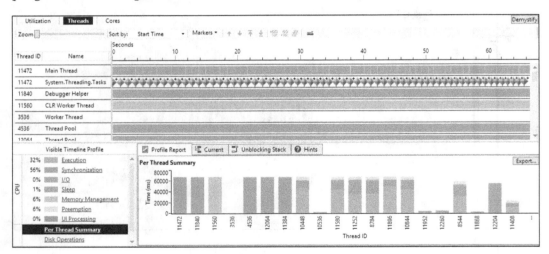

However, the I/O threads report indicates that about half of the program time threads are in the blocked state:

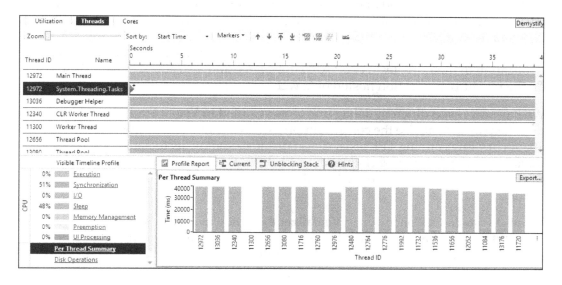

There is a lot of data in this report, and if you run a profiler session to collect concurrency information, you can get even more details. But this is just the starting point where you can see what is going on in the program, and depending on the information received in the report, you can further investigate why the program does not use all the CPU computational power, or why it spends a lot of time in synchronization process.

Summary

In this chapter, we learned about the different stages of application development where we can detect and fix problems in concurrent applications. We reviewed different testing techniques that help to prevent bugs from getting into the application code. We learned to use asynchronous unit tests, host an OWIN Web API application in memory, test HTTP API controllers, and also adapt these tests to run on the real http application hosted on a web server in a test environment.

We have reviewed different debugging tools included in Visual Studio. These tools help us to visualize the concurrent program workflow, show information about currently running TPL tasks, detect deadlocks, allow us to pause and resume threads, see the details of each thread, and help us to use asynchronous call stacks in a comfortable way, so it is clear where the current asynchronous operation has been started.

We also installed a Concurrency Visualizer extension in Visual Studio 2013 and used it to find out what is going on in the concurrent application, how much time the application spends synchronizing, blocking threads, and doing CPU-bound work.

Index

Symbols

4-gigabyte tuning 53
.NET
  concurrent collections 124, 125
.NET 4.0+
  Producer/Consumer pattern 149-152

A

ABA problem 35, 36
acquire fence 29
async/await infrastructure 155
async/await statements 167
asynchronous I/O 194-197
asynchronous patterns
  about 163
  Asynchronous Programming
    Model (APM) 164-167
  Event-based Asynchronous Pattern
    (EAP) 167-171
  Task-based Asynchronous Pattern
    (TAP) 171-173
Asynchronous Programming Model (APM)
  about 164-166
  features 166, 167
async keyword 113
async over sync 200
atomic operations 31
await keyword
  about 235
  working 220
await statement 163

B

Bing
  image downloads, implementing from 99
  URL 99
blocking queue 144
bounded queue 144

C

C# 5.0 built-in support, for asynchrony
  code, enhancing with 108, 109
cache
  implementing, with
    ReaderWriterLockSlim 121, 123
cache aside pattern 121
callbacks
  used, for task cancellation 81-83
C# asynchronous infrastructure
  simulating, with iterators 110-113
class constraint 40
coarse-grained approach
  about 83-86, 60
  selecting 64
coarse-grained locking 124
code coupling 72
common problems
  about 216-220
  solutions 216-220
compare-and-swap (CAS) 130
compiler optimizations 28-30
Component Object Model (COM) 224
concurrency 1

Concurrency Visualizer 250-253
ConcurrentBag<T>
    about 136-139
    using 139
ConcurrentDictionary
    about 125-127
    details, implementing 129, 130
    exclusive lock operations 130-134
    fine-grained lock operations 130-134
    implementation details, using 136
    Lazy<T> 128, 129
    lock-free operations 130, 131
concurrent idioms
    about 155
    parallelism degree, limiting 158-162
    Process Tasks, in Completion
        Order 155-158
    task timeout, setting 162, 163
concurrent patterns 173
ConcurrentQueue<T> 140-142
ConcurrentStack<T> 143
continuation task 70
cooperative multitasking 1
CPU-bound tasks and queues 206
custom awaitable type
    implementing 115, 116
CustomProvider class 123

D

deadlock 5
debugging
    about 244
    call stack window 245, 246
    Enable Just My Code setting 244
    parallel stacks window 248, 249
    Tasks window 247, 248
    threads window 246
double checked locking pattern 48

E

EditBin.exe tool 53
Enqueue method 141

Event-based Asynchronous Pattern (EAP)
    about 167-170
    features 170, 171
exception handling 87-90
exclusive lock operations 134
execution context 221-223

F

fake asynchronous I/O operations 198-203
features, Asynchronous Programming
        Model (APM)
    complicated implementation 166
    coupling, between asynchronous operation
        provider and consumer 167
    low-level pattern 166
    low performance overhead 166
features, Event-based Asynchronous
        Pattern (EAP)
    complicated implementation 171
    coupling, between asynchronous operation
        provider and consumers 171
    high-level pattern 170
    high overhead 170
    intended for UI components 170
features, Task-based Asynchronous
        Pattern (TAP)
    avoidance, of side effects 173
    comfortable to use 173
    high-level 173
    language support, in C#/VB 173
    low overhead 173
    Task and Task<T>, first-class objects 173
fine-grained approach
    about 61
    selecting 64
fine-grained lock operations 132-134
fire-and-forget tasks 113, 114
foreach loop 158
fork/join pattern 173
future 68

G

granularity 60

H

heisenbugs 232
high coupling 72
hyperthreading technology 210

I

image downloads, implementing
    from Bing
  about 99
  C# asynchronous infrastructure, simulating
    with iterators 110-113
  code, enhancing with C# 5.0 built-in
    support 108, 109
  parallel solution, creating with Task Parallel
    Library 105-107
  simple synchronous solution,
    creating 100-104
input/output threads 58
integration tests 239-244
interlocked internals
  working 33
I/O and CPU-bound tasks 191-194
I/O Completion Port (IOCP) 192

L

latency approach, with TPL 83-86
legacy code support scenario 171
load testing 187-191
lock-free algorithms 27
lock-free code
  writing 34, 35
lock-free operations 131
lock-free queue 43-49
lock-free stack 37-42
lock localization 22

locks

locks
  using 5
lock statement 5-8, 120
low coupling 72

M

memory barrier 20, 30
memory model 28-30
message loop 210-216
message pump 212
Monitor class 9-12
mutex synchronization primitive 38

O

only for legacy code support scenario 167
Open Web Interface for .NET (OWIN Web
    API framework) 183-186
optimization strategy
  about 22
  lock localization 22
  shared data minimization 23-25
OS wait objects
  using, with WaitHandle 80

P

Parallel class
  Parallel.Foreach method 92, 93
  Parallel.For method 92, 93
  Parallel.Invoke method 91, 92
  using 90
parallel pipeline
  about 173
  implementing 174-179
parallel programming model 67
parallel programs
  heisenbugs 232
  troubleshooting 231
parallel solution
  creating, with Task Parallel Library 105-107
performance issues 223-227

performance measurement 250
PLINQ 125
preemptive multitasking 1
Producer/Consumer pattern
  about 143, 173
  implementing 144-149
  in .NET 4.0+ 149-152
profiling 250
promise 68

R

race condition
  about 2, 233
  sample 2-5
reader writer lock 12-18
ReaderWriterLockSlim
  used, for implementing cache 121, 123
ready queue 12
real asynchronous I/O operations 198-203
release fence 30
replicable task 92
robust and performant applications
  creating, stages 232
RunLongRunningOperation method 127

S

scalability 182-191
server application
  about 181, 182
  horizontal scalability 182
  scalability 181
  scale vertically 182
  types 181
shared data minimization 23-25
simple synchronous solution
  creating 100-104
Single-Threaded Apartment (STA) 224
spin lock
  about 19
  System.Threading.SpinLock 20-22
  System.Threading.SpinWait 19
  Thread.SpinWait 19

standard collections 120, 121
synchronization context 203-206, 221-223
synchronization primitives 120, 121
System.Threading.Interlocked class 30-32
System.Threading.SpinLock 20, 22
System.Threading.SpinWait 19
System.Threading.Task class 63

T

Tables class
  m_buckets 130
  m_comparer 130
  m_countPerLock 130
  m_locks 130
Task-based Asynchronous Pattern (TAP)
  about 171
  features 173
task-based parallelism 68
task cancellation
  about 76-78
  exception, throwing 79, 80
  flag, checking 78, 79
  OS wait objects, using with WaitHandle 80
  with callbacks 81-83
task composition 68-72
Task Parallel Library (TPL)
  about 61, 99
  parallel solution, creating with 105-107
Task Parallel Library (TPL), features
  about 114
  Task.Delay 115
  Task.Yield 115
task scheduler 68, 93, 96
tasks hierarchy 73-75
tests
  load tests 233
  unit tests 233-239
  writing 232
thread contention 121
thread pool
  using 58, 59

threads
  about 1
  overview 51- 57
Thread.SpinWait 19
TPL task
  completion, awaiting 75, 76

U

UI
  asynchrony, importance 209, 210
UI thread 210-216

V

volatile keyword 28
volatile read 29
volatile write 29

W

wait-free algorithms 27
WaitHandle
  OS wait objects, using with 80
waiting queue 12
while loop 134, 157
Windows Forms 103
worker threads 58
work stealing 136

X

xampp 189

Thank you for buying
Mastering C# Concurrency

About Packt Publishing

Packt, pronounced 'packed', published its first book, *Mastering phpMyAdmin for Effective MySQL Management*, in April 2004, and subsequently continued to specialize in publishing highly focused books on specific technologies and solutions.

Our books and publications share the experiences of your fellow IT professionals in adapting and customizing today's systems, applications, and frameworks. Our solution-based books give you the knowledge and power to customize the software and technologies you're using to get the job done. Packt books are more specific and less general than the IT books you have seen in the past. Our unique business model allows us to bring you more focused information, giving you more of what you need to know, and less of what you don't.

Packt is a modern yet unique publishing company that focuses on producing quality, cutting-edge books for communities of developers, administrators, and newbies alike. For more information, please visit our website at www.packtpub.com.

About Packt Enterprise

In 2010, Packt launched two new brands, Packt Enterprise and Packt Open Source, in order to continue its focus on specialization. This book is part of the Packt Enterprise brand, home to books published on enterprise software – software created by major vendors, including (but not limited to) IBM, Microsoft, and Oracle, often for use in other corporations. Its titles will offer information relevant to a range of users of this software, including administrators, developers, architects, and end users.

Writing for Packt

We welcome all inquiries from people who are interested in authoring. Book proposals should be sent to author@packtpub.com. If your book idea is still at an early stage and you would like to discuss it first before writing a formal book proposal, then please contact us; one of our commissioning editors will get in touch with you.

We're not just looking for published authors; if you have strong technical skills but no writing experience, our experienced editors can help you develop a writing career, or simply get some additional reward for your expertise.

C# Multithreaded and Parallel Programming

ISBN: 978-1-84968-832-1   Paperback: 344 pages

Develop powerful C# applications to take advantage of today's multicore hardware

1. Make use of the latest Visual Studio debugging tools, to manage and debug multiple threads running simultaneously.

2. Learn how to use the Thread, Task, and Parallel libraries in your C# applications.

3. Explore the evolution of multithreaded development in C#, starting with BackgroundWorker classes and moving on to threads and tasks and finally covering Async.

C++ Multithreading Cookbook

ISBN: 978-1-78328-979-0   Paperback: 422 pages

Over 60 recipes to help you create ultra-fast multithreaded applications using C++ with rules, guidelines, and best practices

1. Create multithreaded applications using the power of C++.

2. Upgrade your applications with parallel execution in easy-to-understand steps.

3. Stay up to date with new Windows 8 concurrent tasks.

4. Avoid classical synchronization problems.

Please check **www.PacktPub.com** for information on our titles

Learning Concurrent Programming in Scala

ISBN: 978-1-78328-141-1   Paperback: 366 pages

Learn the art of building intricate, modern, scalable concurrent applications using Scala

1. Design and implement scalable and easy-to-understand concurrent applications.

2. Make the most of Scala by understanding its philosophy and harnessing the power of multicores.

3. Get acquainted with cutting-edge technologies in the field of concurrency, with a particular emphasis on practical, real-world applications.

Mastering Concurrency in Go

ISBN: 978-1-78398-348-3   Paperback: 328 pages

Discover and harness Go's powerful concurrency features to develop and build fast, scalable network systems

1. Explore the core syntaxes and language features that enable concurrency in Go.

2. Understand when and where to use concurrency to keep data consistent and applications non-blocking, responsive, and reliable.

3. A practical approach to utilize application scaffolding to design highly-scalable programs that are deeply rooted in go routines and channels.

Please check **www.PacktPub.com** for information on our titles